Haunted
New York

D0062093

0 11557 03249 9

Haunted New York

Ghosts and Strange Phenomena of the Empire State

Cheri Revai

Illustrations by Heather Adel Wiggins

STACKPOLE
BOOKS

Copyright © 2005 by Stackpole Books

Published by
STACKPOLE BOOKS
5067 Ritter Road
Mechanicsburg, PA 17055
www.stackpolebooks.com

All rights reserved, including the right to reproduce this book or portions thereof in any form or by any means, electronic or mechanical, including photocopying, recording, or by any information storage and retrieval system, without permission in writing from the publisher. All inquiries should be addressed to Stackpole Books.

Printed the United States

10 9 8 7 6 5 4

FIRST EDITION

Design by Beth Oberholtzer
Cover design by Caroline Stover

Library of Congress Cataloging-in-Publication Data

Revai, Cheri, 1963–
    Haunted New York : ghosts and strange phenomena of the Empire State / Cheri Revai.–1st ed.
        p.   cm.
    Includes bibliographical references.
    ISBN-13: 978-0-8117-3249-9 (pbk.)
    ISBN-10: 0-8117-3249-5 (pbk.)
    1. Haunted places—New York (State)   2. Ghosts—New York (State)
I. Title.
BF1472.U6R478   2005
133.1'09747-dc22
                                                     2005009365

To my daughters,
Michelle, Jamie, Katie, and Nikki,
the apples of my eye.

Contents

Contents

Introduction

I JUMPED AT THE OPPORTUNITY TO WRITE THIS BOOK. AFTER THREE years of concentrating heavily on the North Country with my Haunted Northern New York series, I was ready to expand my horizons. I wrote *Haunted Massachusetts: Ghosts and Strange Phenomena of the Bay State,* which was a project I enjoyed immensely. And then I knuckled down and started researching ghost stories for *Haunted New York: Ghosts and Strange Phenomena of the Empire State.* After traveling to every corner of my home state, I narrowed the stories I would use down to a relatively measly number of those I collected. You see, my task was to squeeze details of ghosts and strange phenomena from every region of the state into a forty-thousand-word manuscript—a daunting task, considering the vast number of tales of strange encounters I had to select from.

New York State has eleven distinct tourist regions, but I merged them into six for the purposes of this book: Northern New York, Central New York, Western New York, Southern New York, New York City, and Long Island. Northern New York's claim to fame in a paranormal sense would likely be a tie between Beardslee Castle and Champ, the Lake Champlain Monster. Fort Ontario and the Seneca Hill Ghost are right up there too. The New York State Capitol Building in Albany and the Landmark Theatre in Syracuse are probably Central New York's most famous haunted places. Western New York is most noted for its girl ghost, Tanya, who is said to run the halls of Grand Island's Holiday Inn resort, but everyone knows how haunted Fort Niagara and the USS *The Sullivans* ship-museum are. Southern New York has its still-haunted Sleepy Hollow, as well as Pine Bush, the UFO hot spot of the entire Northeast. New York City and Long Island are in Southern New York as well, but because their combined population amounts to more than 90 percent of the entire state, individual sections of this book are dedicated to each of the two areas. New York City boasts of far too many ghosts to decide which is the most famous, but the apparitions haunting the Belasco Theatre and Chumley's immediately come to mind. Kings Park Psychiatric Center on Long Island has been thoroughly investigated by ghost hunters and ranks right up there on the island's top-ten haunted places, but the region may be even more famous for its Men in Black encounters and other unexplained phenomena, such as the unforgettable spitting cloud of Oyster Bay.

True to its image of diversity in every category, such as ethnicity, culture, population, and landscape, New York State has a broad range of supernatural phenomena as well. We have ghosts and lake monsters, of course. (Doesn't everyone?) But there are also Bigfoot-like creatures, evil black dogs, the legendary Men in Black, UFO sightings and alien encounters, forest gnomes, strange weather anomalies, crop circles, and more. It's a virtual paranormal paradise for ghost lovers, as well as cryptozoologists, parapsychologists, and ufologists.

Cryptozoology, in case you were wondering, is the study of creatures whose existence has not been substantiated. The Empire State has played host to a number of so-called unsubstantiated creatures. Champ, the Lake Champlain monster, tops the state's list of crypto characters, even though he shuns publicity as crypto-creatures inherently do. But there are scores of other mysterious entities in every region of the state that are dying for attention, and I'll tell you just where to find them.

What more can I say? I love New York!

Northern New York

THE ADIRONDACK MOUNTAINS TO THE EAST, THE MIGHTY ST. LAWRENCE River and Lake Ontario to the west, historic Lake Champlain bordering on its northern parameter—Northern New York is a land of plenty. Plenty of geological features, plenty of natural resources, and plenty of ghosts. The only thing missing is a major population center, but that doesn't equate to fewer ghost stories in these parts.

East of the Adirondacks is "America's Fourth Seacoast," the Thousand Islands–Seaway, with its haunted islands and hidden caves, and two hundred miles of the historic Seaway Trail along the St. Lawrence and eastern shores of Lake Ontario. Strategic forts and port towns have been restored along that strip, and battle reenactments are a common sight. Countless visitors to the region have reported seeing what they believed were spectral soldiers at the various forts. Many times they initially thought they were seeing people who were dressed for the part for visitors, but when the soldiers disappeared before their eyes, they quickly decided otherwise.

The vast six-million-acre Adirondack Park encompasses the majority of the northern region of New York State, providing an extraordinary haven of tranquil lakes and spectacular mountain views to which city dwellers can escape. An incredible 2.3 million acres of the Adirondacks have been designated "forever wild." No wonder Bigfoot continues to elude captivity. That's a lot of ground to cover if he's hiding out there somewhere. There have been countless reports of Bigfoot-like "wild men" throughout the area for hundreds of years.

The North Country also has its lake monsters, the most famous being Champ of Lake Champlain, and UFO sightings, such as the ones near the Fort Drum military base. In this region that's so popular among campers and boaters, you just never know what you might encounter "out there."

Beardslee Castle

Long before Augustus Beardslee built his Scottish-style castle on NY Route 5 between Little Falls and St. Johnsville in 1860, a fortified homestead stood on the site. During the French and Indian War in the 1700s, munitions and powder were stored in tunnels designed for that purpose beneath the homestead. Legend has it that a band of Indians sneaked into the tunnels one night in search of the weapons stockpile, but their torches ignited the gunpowder, and the ensuing explosion killed them all. That's one reason why people believe Manheim's Beardslee Castle—now a unique restaurant serving "inspired" American cuisine—is haunted. Two of the three tunnels, used later as part of the Underground Railroad, have since been permanently sealed off. If the band of restless Indian souls were unhappy about their untimely deaths in the tunnels, imagine their displeasure when, in the late 1800s, Augustus's son Guy Beardslee returned to his family's estate with Sioux war artifacts. He had obtained these tomahawks, knives, and war bonnets while commissioned at Fort Niobrara in Nebraska, where the army was taking land from the Sioux. Talk about rubbing salt on an open wound.

Restless Native American spirits may not be the only ones still roaming the grounds. Back in the mid-1950s, a previous owner hanged himself in an area now used as a side entrance to the castle. After years of operating what he called "The Manor," he had become terminally ill and attempted suicide several times. He finally succeeded, but perhaps he's having second thoughts about leaving just yet, for some allegedly have seen his apparition right where he took his last breath. Other specters reportedly seen include a male figure dressed in a top hat and black suit; a transparent figure, believed to be Captain Beardslee, carrying a brightly lit lantern on the roadside; and an X-ray or skeleton ghost, whose bones were clearly visible; a blond woman wearing a long dress in the ladies' room; a woman in similar attire carrying a bed tray up a nonexistent stairway; and even a ghostly quartet dining by candlelight that disappeared moments after being spotted. There is no shortage of apparitions in the gloriously haunted castle. And that's what made it so appealing to the History Channel, which included a segment on Beardslee Castle in October 1999 as part of its Haunted History series.

Besides the hodgepodge of apparitions drifting about, the castle's spirits have made their presence known throughout the grounds and surrounding properties in ways ranging from the very subtle to the blatantly tangible and the benign to the incredibly reckless. Visitors have seen shadows on walls where nobody was walking by, and heard footsteps, strange voices, and whispers. Three employees once heard a very loud, chilling scream reverberating through the entire castle, sending them racing for the door. It's not uncommon for an employee to hear his or her name spoken or whispered by an unfamiliar voice. Many people have seen strange lights of different colors drifting and darting through the rooms and flitting across the lawn and road. In fact, an unusually high number of vehicle accidents have occurred on the road in front of the property over the years, sometimes blamed on bizarre lights that emerged from the woods and blinded the drivers, causing the death of at least one man. Whether the ill-intentioned lights were orbs of pure spirit energy or the ghost lantern carried by Captain Beardslee, who is said to occasionally wander along the road at night, or whether they were something else altogether, everyone agrees that they were not of this world.

The staff has experienced poltergeist-type behavior, finding tables and chairs flipped over when they arrive in the morning, seeing silverware flying across the kitchen of the restaurant or bottles and glasses breaking out of the blue, and hearing strange disembodied voices that seem to encircle them. Several employees once used a Ouija board to try to summon the spirits of the dead, but they were quickly thwarted in their efforts when the lights went out on their own and one of the employees felt a sudden shove on his chest from something unseen that threw him across the room.

Another group of employees was once chased from the castle by grotesque howling.

The owners admit they've had people quit in midshift and never return to the building, but they stress on their website: "Augustus Beardslee's Castle is a beautiful and compelling building that has a powerful, true sense of place. Unique, captivating, and mysterious as well, we are honored to share this castle with our guests, from this dimension and any other." They leave it up to the customers of their fine restaurant, which is open year-round, to explore the grounds for themselves and decide whether the elegant castle and dining establishment feels haunted.

Burrville Cider Mill

Many of the ghost stories I write are works in progress, in that they continue to unfold long after the story goes to press. In the first book of my Haunted Northern New York series, I wrote about the Burrville Cider Mill, on the Plank Road off NY Route 12 about five minutes southeast of Watertown. A lot has happened since, and by now its owners probably have enough paranormal incidents under their belts to fill an entire book.

The Burrville Cider Mill, one of Jefferson County's oldest establishments, is owned and operated by the Steiner family, Greg Sr., Cynthia, Greg Jr., and Tina. It was built at the bottom of a waterfall on Sandy Creek in 1801 and for many years was called Burr's Mills, for its sawmill and gristmill. In 1996, the Steiners purchased the two-hundred-year-old mill, even though they had been told it was haunted. It wasn't long before they were welcomed by two unique gentlemen: Homer Rebb (at your service), the ghost of a former owner; and Captain John Burr, the ghost of the town's and mill's namesake, and the wilder of the two. Burr is said to have stolen from ships on Lake Ontario so that he could sell his hot items to soldiers at Sackets Harbor.

One of the first unusual things that happened to the Steiners in their new enterprise was the disappearance of a twenty-five-pound bag of sugar that has never been found. Tina Steiner left the bag out in the back room at the end of the day, then locked up and left. She was the last one out, and the place was secure. But the next morning when she opened up, she noticed that the bag was gone.

It had been there when she left, of that she was sure. And none of the other Steiners had anything to do with it. Was a bag of sugar sold around that time by a scoundrel that looked like a pirate from yesteryear?

Besides the missing sugar, the Steiners have experienced many other incidents of a ghostly nature. They often hear the sounds of heavy objects dropping in the attic and lightweight hard, plastic balls bouncing across the wooden floor, when nothing can be seen to account for the sound. They have also heard the sound of the old double cider press Homer built in the basement, as if it's turning its own wheels on their metal rack. Objects malfunction, so the women have taken to asking Homer to fix them, and he usually obliges. Once a gentleman, always a gentleman.

As for the Captain, Cindy Steiner once saw the reflection of a man wearing heavy black wool pants and brown leather work boots in the glass cooler door of the mill, but when she turned around to face the intruder, he was gone. A customer was taking photographs of the mill's exterior one day, making sure to wait until nobody was in the way. But when she got her photographs developed, she was perplexed—and a bit thrilled—to see a man standing by the door to the sorting room, looking very much like one would expect Captain Burr to look, with full beard, boots to his knees, and cradling his arm as though it was holding something or somehow disabled. The man was a bit blurrier than the rest of the picture—as if he wasn't quite all there.

The cigars that people occasionally smell when nobody is smoking can probably be blamed on Captain Burr, as well. One such cigar, described as an old-fashioned stogie, was found in the building, covered in cobwebs, as if it had been dropped there out of the blue from another dimension. And it was discovered right after the area had been cleaned and freshly painted. Round candy balls are moved around and specifically placed in certain locations, lights flicker, and things often go bump in the night . . . and in the daytime.

A local television crew was doing a news special on haunted locations in Northern New York in April 2001, when they got more than they hoped for at the mill. It happened to be the cameraman's birthday, and he wasn't ashamed to ask out loud for a little something extra for a birthday bonus. Sure enough, when the cameraman was interviewing Tina Steiner on videotape inside the mill, a swinging door opened behind her in a very slow and deliberate way, and then closed very slowly. It might have been explainable had anyone else been in that room at the time, but nobody was. It was just the cameraman and Mrs. Steiner. At the time, the cameraman didn't see the door; he was concentrating on the person he was interviewing. When he got back to the office and played the tape, he saw the door open and close, and then he called me up, barely able to contain his excitement. The incident thrilled the news program's viewers.

When I was signing books at Borders in Watertown a year and a half ago, two young newlyweds told me they had recently exchanged wedding vows at the Burrville Cider Mill. With the brilliant foliage and waterfall as a backdrop, it's a gorgeous place to marry in the fall. They had read about the mill being haunted in my book and thought it would be wonderful if something paranormal occurred during their wedding ceremony. They weren't disappointed. Photograph after photograph had floating orbs, unexplained mists and streaks, and other anomalies often attributed to spirit energy. The newlyweds couldn't have been more thrilled with their wedding memories.

Cindy Steiner shared another recent incident with me. She said, "After reading your book, some of my cousins asked for a special tour of the building to hopefully get a glimpse of the ghost. Lorna, one of the cousins, said that while she was upstairs, something played with her long hair, but she was at the back of the group. Nobody was behind her. When we were in the store area, someone stepped on her foot and also called her name two or three times (this was only heard by her). Lorna's husband was taking pictures during the tour, and all the pictures with me in them are blurry. They had owned this camera for quite some time and had taken hundreds of pictures, and never had that happen, before or since."

Champ, the Lake Champlain Monster

No compilation of paranormal phenomena would be complete without mention of Lake Champlain's famous and painfully shy lake creature, Champ, New York State's darling of cryptozoological critters. So legendary is he that he's been featured on such popular shows as *Today, Unsolved Mysteries,* and *Sightings,* as well as a Discovery channel special devoted entirely to him, called *America's Loch Ness Monster.* Champ looks and acts much like his Scottish counterpart, Nessie, according to hundreds of eyewitnesses from 1873 to the present time. Both are so-called lake monsters, for lack of a specific scientific name for them, at least until one can be captured and positively identified. Both lurk in deep, cold-water lakes, ever elusive to the inquiring public, as sea and lake serpents always seem to be. But if you do see one, it will be unmistakable. To my untrained eye, Champ looks just like a water-dwelling, long-necked dinosaur, and apparently he has cousins all over the state. Sightings of snake- and serpent-like lake creatures have been reported for more than two hundred years, not only in Lake Champlain, but also in Lake Erie, Lake Ontario, Onondaga Lake, and even the St. Lawrence River.

Western New York's paranormal expert and author Mason Winfield chronicles the sightings in the following order in *Spirits of the Great Hill:* In Lake Erie, a giant snake more than sixteen feet long chased a duck hunter in 1793. A black eel-like creature thirty to forty feet long was spotted on Lake Ontario in 1817. A similar creature was reported by a ship's crew in 1880. In 1892, an even larger serpent was seen by the crew of a schooner leaving Buffalo. Four years later, a large serpent with a doglike head was seen near Fort Erie, and in July 1900, there were three separate sightings of a lake creature approximately fifty feet long off Stony Point, near Elmwood Beach. Onondaga Lake was home to a lake monster named Mosqueto, which was believed to have killed people. As long ago as 700 B.C., Lake Ontario reportedly harbored a great horned snake whose smell proved toxic. Several years ago, a few residents of the small shoreline community of Waddington, New York, claimed that they had seen a Champ-like creature in the St. Lawrence River. Explorer Samuel de Champlain, who discovered Lake Champlain, was mistakenly believed to have been the first European to have spotted Champ in the lake. But the lake serpent he described having seen in the 1600s was in the St. Lawrence River.

The *Plattsburgh Republican* of July 24, 1819, had one of the earliest documented accounts of a Champ-like creature in Lake Champlain: "Captain Crum was aboard a scow on Bulwagga Bay the

previous Thursday morning when he reported a black monster, about 187 feet long and with a head resembling a 'sea horse' that reared over 15 feet out of the water." In 1873, the *New York Times* reported that a railroad crew had spotted an enormous serpent in Lake Champlain. Later that year, the Clinton County sheriff reported seeing a similar creature, and a month later, tourists onboard a steamship on the lake claimed their boat was nearly capsized when it ran into a Champ-like creature. Circus magnate P. T. Barnum, who coined the phrase "There's a sucker born every minute," offered $5,000—an extremely large sum of money in 1873—to anyone who could bring him the hide of the Champlain serpent to include in his World's Fair Show.

A hundred years later, Champlain's lake monster was officially named Champ. The most famous photograph of Champ is an Instamatic picture taken by Sandra Mansi while her family was picnicking on the shoreline. She claimed that a strange turbulence in the water caught her eye because her children were swimming nearby, and when she looked closely at it, she saw what looked like a huge creature with a small head, humped back, and long neck. As the children were rushed out of the water, she snapped the photograph. A friend who saw it in their family photo album persuaded them to show it to Champ expert Joe Zarzynski, who wrote a book called *Champ: Beyond the Legend,* and the rest was history. "By any standard," says Jerome Clark, author of the book *Unexplained!,* "the Mansi photograph remains a genuine mystery and a serious obstacle to any effort to reduce the Champ phenomenon to mundane causes."

By the end of the twentieth century, so many people had seen Champ that even the law acknowledged that the Lake Champlain monster existed. Just as an endangered species would be protected by law, so too was Champ. Resolutions were passed on both sides of Lake Champlain in 1982 and 1983, and Port Henry, New York, declared its waters a safe haven for the creature. The small village's welcoming sign says, "Village of Port Henry—Home of Champ." The twenty-first century has already had a few newsworthy Champ sightings. A November 26, 2000, photograph of an anomaly in the water by a Willsboro, New York, resident appeared in the *Press Republican* the following month. It was the sixteenth Champ sighting that year. The photographer said she was looking out over the water from her residence and noticed that the seagulls were making a commotion over something. Upon closer inspection, she saw a long, straight form partially emerged from the water that stayed very still for about fifteen minutes. When it finally moved, it "humped up in the middle," she said, and "left a little wake behind it."

The most recent sighting at the time of this writing occurred in July 2004. According to a *Press Republican* article of August 2, five vacationers from Maryland had a "close encounter with Champ." A man and four of his grandchildren were fishing in the middle of the lake when they heard a seagull crying and saw it flapping around in the water. It looked as if three fish were trying to get it, but it turned out to be three large humps from the same dark black, snakelike creature that undulated through the water. A man who had never believed in Champ or the Loch Ness Monster, the grandfather from Maryland became a believer that day.

When it comes to the Lake Champlain Monster, seeing is believing, and based on the mounting evidence of photographs, video footage, eyewitness statements, and sonar readings of the lake bottom, it would be hard not to believe that there's something out there, somewhere, in the 400-foot-deep, 109-mile-long lake. Perhaps Fauna Communications Research, a North Carolina–based institute studying Champ, puts it best: "What we can say is that there is a creature in the lake that produces bio-sonar. We have no idea what it is." And the not knowing is exactly what keeps this legend alive.

Fort Ontario

At least four specific ghosts are believed to haunt Oswego's Fort Ontario on a regular basis, and many others seem to have passed through once or twice. I wouldn't hazard a guess as to the numbers, but suffice it to say that the fort appears to be exceptionally haunted. But what would you expect in a place where bloody battles, starvation, hypothermia, and incurable diseases took hundreds of lives; men fought duels and committed murders unrelated to battle; and soldiers were forced to eat their own to survive? That's right . . . cannibalism, right here in Northern New York.

Fort Ontario was built about 1755 on the banks of Lake Ontario. At various times in its history, it was occupied by the British,

French, and Americans. The United States has held it the longest, since 1796. It is now a museum owned and operated by the New York State Office of Parks, Recreation, and Historic Preservation, which has authentically restored it to depict life at the fort in 1868, a relatively benign period compared with others the site has seen.

The winter of 1752 proved especially unkind at the fort. In fact, the British troops then occupying it became so desperate for warmth and nourishment in the harsh conditions that they enchained their commanding officer and left the site in search of food at a nearby village. But a blizzard hampered their efforts, so they returned to the fort dejected. Before long, in order to survive the brutal winter, the men were forced to kill and eat their comrades. The unforgiving winter of 1755 saw mounds of frozen and starved bodies. The Colonial wars and the War of 1812, likewise, resulted in hundreds of deaths. What's amazing is not the fact that Fort Ontario is haunted by a few ghosts, but that it's not haunted by hundreds. The number of lives prematurely terminated here is extremely high.

According to an article called "'Ghosts of Old Fort Ontario' Program Set" in the *Valley News* of October 19, 2002, the ghost stories associated with Fort Ontario started around 1900 in an effort by one Sergeant Fawdry to scare children away. Although it's rarely possible to determine with certainty the identity of a ghost, Fawdry put names to two alleged Fort Ontario ghosts. These monikers have stuck, though the ghostly identities are based solely on the opinion of Sergeant Fawdry and the appearance of the uniforms observers describe the ghosts as wearing. Fawdry told of a British lieutenant named Basil Dunbar, who haunted the fort after losing a duel in 1759. Some recent sightings have Dunbar's ghost wandering about the site dazed and confused, as if he doesn't realize he's dead. Fawdry also talked about Corporal Fykes, who was actually an American loyalist who died in 1782 from disease, not a British soldier who died of hunger—a rumor Fawdry apparently spread for dramatic effect or out of pure ignorance. According to Lynda Lee Macken in *Empire Ghosts*, Fykes's ghost has appeared to every new regiment for more than a hundred years, and whenever seen, the witnesses have reported a rapid decrease in room temperature. The bodies of both Fykes and Dunbar are buried in the Post Cemetery.

Another ghost has been seen in a blue uniform like those worn after the Civil War. An apparition of a female figure has been "felt" by psychics, and her image may have been caught on film by a team of paranormal investigators in 1998. That same group of people, New York State's representatives in the American Ghost Society, recorded unusual electro-magnetic field (EMF) readings and temperature drops, especially in the men's barracks, where an argument had once led to murder. While they were investigating, they heard a loud bang reverberating throughout the grounds, and no source for the sound was ever found. They also took a number of photographs that seem to depict spirit energy. All this has led them to believe that Fort Ontario is indeed haunted.

The fort's youngest ghost is a baby sometimes heard crying and giggling. A ball of light that may be the spirit of a former guard flits about the night watchman's head and post, alternating between blue and green. After Fort Ontario went from being an important defensive post to a training post in 1903, it was guarded by just one sergeant, who also acted as caretaker. Perhaps the courteous little ball of energy is there to assist the watchman through his long, lonely nights at the fort, when doors slam shut for no apparent reason and footsteps resonate where nobody appears to be walking.

Though it was decommissioned after World War II, Fort Ontario certainly seems to have remained very active.

Graveyard Ghosts

I've heard stories about ghosts in cemeteries all over New York's North Country, especially in my own hometown of Massena. It was here at Calvary Cemetery that a groundskeeper complained of seeing a dark-clad fellow grinning at him just before the man disappeared before his eyes, and another caretaker was approached by a woman who seemed as if she was about to ask him a question before she floated straight through a gravestone and evaporated into thin air.

At the Pine Grove Cemetery on Beach Street in Massena, Joan Szarka and her son got the scare of a lifetime one evening as they strolled down the narrow road toward the back of the 1872 graveyard with their dog. They were talking about a man named Dragon, who was buried nearby. His lonely gravestone had attracted their attention earlier because of the unusual name etched on it, so they did some fact-finding and learned that he had been killed, but they wondered how. Just as they were passing by his grave, the wind picked up, their dog became tense and started to whine, and Joan's son thought he saw an apparition while feeling a chill go straight through him. Then they heard a creepy whisper directly behind them saying "Turn around." They were certain they were the only people in the graveyard at that moment, so they did not comply with the sinister demand. Instead, they hurried out of the cemetery, shaken but more determined than ever to learn about the man named Dragon. It turned out that he was a local businessman and womanizer who had been shot in the face and chest in a hunting accident in the 1940s. The cause of death was ruled accidental, and the case was closed. Joan has often wondered why she was told to turn around and face the man's grave. What would she have seen if she had? Did he want her to see him? What was so important that he spoke those two words from beyond the grave?

North Country native Chris Sharlow, author of *Shutter*, a book of his spirit photographs, has had a number of interesting encounters with ghosts in graveyards. He knows they're there because he has felt their presence, sometimes physically, and has taken hundreds of photographs of various forms of spirit energy and apparitions in cemeteries from New York to Maine, where he currently resides. One particular incident that stands out in his mind is when he and a friend both began taking photographs at the same time. Suddenly, sparks flew out in every direction, and in the illuminated mist, a form started taking shape. Then he felt someone leaning on him, as if pushing him away—and it wasn't his friend, who had already skedaddled.

When my first book was published in 2002, ghostly images captured by Sharlow stared back at readers from the cover, and reactions ran the gamut from amazement to disbelief. One image showed a streak of red shooting up from a gravestone with a very clear, very angry red face at the top of it. That now famous photograph was taken at Pine Grove #2, in a portion of the otherwise tidy cemetery where many of the stones are in ruins. Pine Grove #2 is a sprawling, sunny cemetery technically in the township of Norfolk, but on Massena's Cook Street.

In 1955, during construction of the St. Lawrence–FDR Power Project and the Seaway, it was necessary to relocate many of the graves from nineteen cemeteries in the Barnhart Island area to Pine Grove #2. According to the 1958 *Report on Cemetery Relocation*, written by Uhl, Hall, and Rich: "Many of these cemeteries were small family plots on old farms which had received very little care or maintenance. Many tombstones were broken beyond repair." The larger Episcopal Diocese Cemetery on the north side of Barnhart Island had 102 bodies—many from the Barnhart family for whom the island was named—that had to be relocated to Pine Grove #2. The Barnhart section of the cemetery is set off by wrought-iron fencing and has yielded a number of photographs that appear to show spirits, including Chris Sharlow's award-winning *Red Face*. Several legends are associated with the relocation of the Barnhart graves, including stories of claw marks on the insides of rotting caskets, as if people had been accidentally buried alive, which did happen, by the way, before the development of advanced medical equipment to confirm death. It was also reported that the condition of many caskets was so poor that they crumbled during removal, so the bodies and caskets and broken tombstones were all thrown into dump trucks in a jumbled heap and were buried at Pine Grove #2 in quite the same manner. You might think there would be a disgruntled spirit or two.

Melodie Rogers is another North Country resident and spirit photographer who has had many unusual cemetery experiences. She based her first novel, a paranormal horror piece called *Followed by Death*, on a mysterious ghostlike figure she captured on film twice in different areas of the same cemetery in Fort Covington. Her photographs can be seen in my third book, *Still More Haunted Northern New York*. She had a frightening experience while attempting to capture ghosts on film at the Massena Center Cemetery. She was taking pictures with her digital camera, pointing it randomly into the darkness, and was starting to get a creepy feeling, though she didn't know why. She had just decided to call it quits for the night and was about to take her last picture when she saw a huge glow before her eyes. She managed to take the picture, and then got out of there. When she downloaded the images onto her computer later that night, her last photograph showed a large orb with a face in it.

The town of Massena was established in 1802, and its first death occurred that same year, so the town's first cemetery was created at

Massena Center. The old portion of the cemetery holds the remains of at least three Revolutionary War soldiers, eighteen Civil War soldiers, and many of Massena's earliest settlers. The land on which it is located is adjacent to the Grasse River and may once have been an Indian burial ground. Several Indian settlements dotted the town's three main rivers before the first European settlers arrived, and they likely buried their dead nearby. Many Native American tribes believed that there are places on the earth that contain invisible portals to the spirit world, where the deceased would most easily find their way to the Great Spirit, so they chose the location of their burial grounds on the advice of their tribal shaman, whom they thought could perceive the other side. If there is a portal at Massena, it would explain the vast number of spirit photographs—including apparitions, orbs, and maybe even an actual portal itself—that Chris Sharlow and Melodie Rogers have taken there.

But Massena isn't alone in its haunted cemeteries. The Sheepfold Cemetery on Route 26 near Fort Drum is also called the POW cemetery because of the very clear row of prisoner-of-war gravestones between two large trees, visible from the road. A soldier once flagged down a woman on the side of that roadway, right near the cemetery, during a blinding snowstorm, but he fled on foot into the woods as she got closer. She was concerned that there had been an accident and he needed assistance, so she waited with her two young children for him to return from the woods, but he never did. She found out the next day that the cemetery is known to be haunted, and others have seen mysterious soldiers vanish there too.

Encountering ghosts in cemeteries can be downright scary, but seeing the spirit of a loved one can bring relief and release. One young lady was having great difficulty letting go after her father died. His body was placed in a vault at the Fairview Cemetery in Canton to await a spring burial. Shortly after the funeral, the woman drove to the cemetery to be near him. She pulled right up in front of the vault, trying to get as close as she could, and started crying. When she finally looked up, something caught her attention in her rearview mirror: Her father was standing there waving. He looked healthy, even though he had lost both legs and his vision to diabetes before he died. He was young and vibrant again, and he was motioning for her to move on. She left that day with a much better acceptance of his passing. She was now at peace because she understood that he was at peace.

Skene Manor

High on a mountain overlooking the village of Whitehall and Lake Champlain sits the legendary Skene Manor. It was designed in 1874 by the architectural firm of Issac Hobbes in Philadelphia for New York State judge Joseph Potter and his wife, Catherine, on property once owned by the man who had founded Skenesborough in 1756, Colonel Philip Skene. Skene was granted the land, which included Skene Mountain, by the British Crown as a reward for his military service. Skene used money from his wife Catherine's yearly dowry to help pay for the house. She was suspicious that her husband might squander her wealth if she died first, so she had her will written explicitly to provide an annual annuity to her husband, only as long as her body remained above ground.

According to the historian for Whitehall Skene Manor Preservation, Inc., a story from the 1940s implied that it didn't take the clever colonel long to figure out that he could avoid losing the annuity simply by having his wife's body embalmed (in vinegar, they say) and propped up in the basement in a lead coffin. That singular act led to many future generations of ghost stories about Catherine Skene. In fact, Skene placed her body into a lead coffin and put it in a storage chamber, as he had promised her he would take her remains home to England.

Colonel Skene fled to Canada in 1777, leaving his wife's body in the basement. It was discovered by invading troops, who stole her jewelry, including a large ring she had proudly shown off while alive. They left her body to be found by others, who buried her somewhere on the property. A hundred years later, Judge Potter tore down the Skene homestead to make way for what is now called Skene Manor. The mansion was constructed on the hallowed ground where Catherine Skene is believed to have been buried, and ghost stories have run rampant ever since.

The mansion passed through many hands over the years, but it became most famous during its time as a restaurant. A previous enterprising owner played Catherine's story to the hilt by placing a coffin behind the bar in plain view, surrounded by a stone fountain.

He rigged the coffin to have a fake hand, wearing a ring alleged to be Catherine's, move when he pulled on a string, causing more than one heavy drinker to leave the place wide-eyed and unwittingly spreading untrue rumors of Catherine's bejeweled hand manifesting before his very eyes at the bar. For many years, people—even those who hadn't been drinking—reported seeing a ghost presumed to be Catherine, wearing a long dress and a large ring on her right hand. Others saw only little balls of unexplained light flitting about the grounds.

Another scintillating tale—and I emphasize that it *is* a tale—had the Skenes' housekeeper falling in love with the colonel and one day murdering Catherine Skene, hiding her body somewhere in the house, and telling the colonel that his wife had run off on him while he was away for a few days. The stories, true and otherwise, involving the death and disappearance of Catherine Skene are perhaps even more entertaining than the ghost stories associated with her.

Skene Manor passed through the hands of various owners before going into a period of abandonment and neglect. Finally a Connecticut man made an offer several years ago to purchase the property, planning to disassemble it stone by stone, but a group of local people calling themselves SOS—Save Our Skene—came to the rescue and bought it to restore it to peak splendor. Today the first and second floors are being renovated, and the manor is open to the public for tours Friday, Saturday, and Sunday, from mid-April to Christmas. The ghost of Catherine may still be around.

The Gougou

Believe it or not, New York has been plagued by Bigfoot sightings since before the earliest Europeans settled in the region. French explorer Samuel de Champlain got a lesson in cryptozoology from the various Native American tribes he met as he traveled up the St. Lawrence River in Northern New York in 1603. They told him of a hideous cave-dwelling creature that was big and hairy and human-like. They called the feared beast Gougou. Champlain called the legend "un monster épouvantable." Both he and the natives believed it was an agent of Satan himself.

The following translation is from Champlain's French journal logs called *Des Savages* written in 1603. Champlain kept careful notes of his explorations of the St. Lawrence River. His journal is generally believed to be the first document ever to contain a report about the man-beast we've come to know as Bigfoot, though some think Champlain is describing a monstrous sea creature that dwelt in the river instead. You can decide:

There is another strange thing worthy of narration, which many savages have assured me was true; this is, that near Chaleur Bay, towards the south, lies an island where makes his abode a dreadful monster, which the savages call Gougou. They told me it has the form of a woman, but most hideous . . . it has often devoured many savages. . . . This monster makes horrible noises in that island, and when they speak of him it is with utterly strange terror and many have assured me that they have seen him. Even Sieur Pervert from St. Malo told me that, while going in search of mines, he passed so near the haunt of this frightful beast, that he and all those on board his vessel heard strange hissings from the noise it made, and that the savages he had with him told him it was the same creature, and were so afraid that they hid themselves wherever they could, for fear it should come to carry them off. And what makes me believe what they say, is the fact that all the savages in general fear it, and tell such strange stories of it, that if I were to record all they say, it would be considered untrue; but I hold that this is the dwelling-place of some devil that torments them in the manner described. This is what I have learned about this Gougou.

Does a Gougou still hiss and lurk along the riverbanks of the St. Lawrence? Consider this: While camping on the shore of the St. Lawrence River at a remote spot near the Town Beach in Massena some twenty years ago, several young men were terrified to hear a dreadful-sounding beast circling their tent. They were too afraid to even peek outside to see if it was a practical jokester. It sounded horrible, like a rabid animal or a madman. One of the young men said it sounded just like what he would have expected a Tasmanian devil to sound like.

More recently, a group of teenage girls split up into two vehicles and headed out for a leisurely drive to Hawkins Point, on the Robinson Bay Road along the St. Lawrence River in Massena. At some point, the first carload of girls noticed that the other car was no longer behind them, so they turned back to see if they could find their friends. There was no sign of them anywhere, so the lead car went back to the house from which they had started. The other car was already there, and the girls that had been in it were near hysterics. They had been following the first car, when they noticed beside the road some sort of creature that they had never seen before. It looked like a giant, hairy, unsightly person—but it wasn't. Whatever it was so terrified the young girls that the driver spun the car around to get out of there, barely touching the brakes as she sped home. It seems the Gougou, or a descendant or cousin, may still be alive and well, hiding somewhere along the St. Lawrence River in Massena.

The Seneca Hill Ghost

There seems to be a paranormal disturbance on Oswego's Seneca Hill, and contrary to popular belief, it doesn't come out only on Halloween. An apparition of a frightened woman, often with a young girl in tow, has been seen many times over the past hundred years, running as if she's fleeing in terror. The manifestation has been seen all over Seneca Hill and reported repeatedly.

Area residents are all familiar with the stories of the apparition, even if they haven't witnessed it themselves. One woman said the woman was wearing Pilgrim-type clothing, including a white bonnet and basket. The sight was so unusual in an area where there are no houses for miles that she did a double-take in her rearview mirror as she drove by, but the strange woman who had been there only a second before had completely vanished. Others have seen the terrified-looking woman hurriedly pulling a young girl about six years of age along on the side of the road. That woman has been described as wearing a high-necked dress, and both she and the child were barefoot. Some people have seen her close enough to notice the look of terror on her face as she raced past them. And one man was startled to see the strange manifestation run, out of the blue, right in front of his car, up onto a porch, and into a house. When he mentioned how strange it was to his wife, who was sitting in the passenger seat beside him, she said she hadn't seen any woman.

Nobody has been able to find a reason for the apparent haunting. No murders or tragic accidents involving a woman and child have been documented in that specific area. Perhaps something occurred long before our time. But even though nobody knows who she was, everybody knows of her ghost.

The Whitehall Creature

"Police are investigating reports of a large, unidentified creature seen last week in the town of Whitehall. The first sighting of the creature, which some have referred to as the notorious 'Bigfoot,' was reported last Tuesday by Marty Paddock of Whitehall and Paul Gosselin of Low Hampton." The front-page article in the August 30, 1976, issue of the Glens Falls *Post-Star,* titled "Officers Track Creature," went on to describe the ordeal faced by two hapless young men a week earlier. They were near Abair Road on their way to go camping, when they saw a huge, human-shaped form on the side of the road. So they turned around and went back to get a better look. As they did, they heard what sounded like a woman screaming or a pig squealing. Gosselin loaded his gun, and they again turned their truck around so he could get a shot at it, if necessary. Suddenly the creature lunged toward the truck, and Gosselin told Paddock to hightail it out of there. They reported the creature to the police, but nobody believed them. Then they took another friend back with them, and all three of them witnessed the creature this time. It was standing very still, all eight or so feet of it, weighed between three hundred and four hundred pounds, and was covered with coarse brown hair. But its most prominent feature, as if its size and hairiness weren't enough, was its big red eyes. After the three reported it to the police station, eight officers followed them back to the site, including Gosselin's own father, an off-duty police sergeant at the time. As they knelt in the field, waiting for the creature to reappear, Gosselin and his father heard a powerful scream. A sheriff saw something strange lurking along the fence and asked what the heck it was, but he later denied that he'd seen anything for fear of ridicule.

Everyone who did see the creature that night, and for many nights thereafter, agreed as to its size. It appeared to be seven or eight feet tall and a good three hundred pounds, at the very least. Its eyes were memorable to those who found themselves close enough to notice them. And it could really scream, especially if it felt cornered . . . or even if it just sensed that it was being pursued.

The morning after the initial incident took place, Gosselin and his brother returned to the scene and found tracks and impressions. One footprint measured nineteen and a half inches long, and whatever made it had a five-foot stride.

Several nights later, other area residents, including a schoolteacher and a deputy sheriff, saw the same thing, or something remarkably similar. Like the young men who first saw it, the teacher and the sheriff were also ridiculed. But they refused to renege on their story. Too many people had seen or heard something very much out of the ordinary to ignore it—something that couldn't be explained as anything other than paranormal.

According to the "Capsule of Summary of Cases" in *Monsters of the North Woods*, in 1959 a farmer sighted a bearlike creature standing on two legs. In 1975, a Skeen Valley Country Club owner came face-to-face with an eight-foot-tall, slothlike creature. Later that year, a police sergeant and his brother heard an eerie high-pitched screech while hunting near Abair Road and Route 22A. August 1976 brought the wave of sightings that began with those of Paddock and Gosselin, followed by many others. In 1977, a grandmother who was driving down Fish Hill Road saw what looked like a stump in a field. She did a double-take when she saw the "stump" stand up and walk away. It was an extremely large, honey-colored creature. In 1978, an "inhuman scream" was heard outside one resident's house. The next year, a couple people were stunned to see a large creature step casually right over a fence. In 1982, two policemen saw a Bigfoot-type creature cross state Route 22 near the Washington County Highway Department garage. In 1983, strange footprints were found by the Whitehall Dump. And 1984 saw several reports of unnerving laughing screams and sightings of an eight-foot-tall creature.

But it was the Paddock-Gosselin encounter with Bigfoot in 1976 that seemed to really get the ball rolling. Even the police sergeant didn't know how to respond to the situation. He was wise to leave it at this: "I'm not saying this is a monster or anything else, but there is something out there, and it's no animal that belongs in the northern part of this state." Such is the basis for cryptozoology.

UFOs over Fort Drum

At 6:31 P.M. on December 15, 1998, CNN broadcast live footage, using a night-vision video camera, of a triangular pattern of lights hovering over downtown Baghdad during Operation Desert Fox. NBC also aired a news report in which the unusual object stood out amid the usual chaos of the Baghdad night sky at that time. In fact, one individual who saw the newscast said the V-shaped object was very definite and striking because, unlike the green tracer fire constantly shooting across the black night sky, it remained fairly still.

Almost three weeks earlier, the New York State branch of the Mutual UFO Network (MUFON) received reports of similarly shaped objects passing over Evans Mills, a small town just outside the Fort Drum Military Reservation boundary, and Perch Lake, a bit farther west near I-81. Fort Drum is an army post in Northern New York that was a staging area for Operation Desert Fox. Heavy UFO activity was reported by a woman living on Perch Lake. She told a MUFON New York member that triangular craft had appeared in the local skies. She described what she saw as similar to a "Pine Bush" (a Hudson Valley UFO hot spot) triangle that moved slowly over the trees and across the lake before vanishing. According to the UFO Roundup website: "A teenager from the local Civil Air Patrol (CAP) told the woman that they have also spotted a craft over Evans Mills. Within the last few weeks, the woman has regularly observed a bluish light with a small red streak at its center." She had watched the UFO hover over her property and the adjacent vacant land for hours.

Could it be that extraterrestrials were watching Operation Desert Fox unfold? Or is it that at least some unidentified flying objects are unidentified only by the general public, but the government knows what they are?

Central New York

FOR THE PURPOSES OF THIS BOOK, CENTRAL NEW YORK CONSISTS OF the Capital-Saratoga District and the Central-Leatherstocking regions combined. Further, it includes the city of Syracuse, which technically (according to several sources) lies within the Finger Lakes region of Western New York on some charts. Many natives consider Central New York synonymous with Syracuse, so you will read about the ghosts at Syracuse's City Hall and Landmark Theatre, as well as Onondaga Lake's bloodthirsty monster, in the following pages.

The Capital District, as you might expect, is as all-American as apple pie. Albany, the state capital, is actually the oldest continuous settlement of the original thirteen colonies. Saratoga is a gem of New York history as well, with more than seven hundred places listed on the National Register of Historic Places and nearly as many ghosts to boot, judging from the tales told by regional authors on the topic. The Central-Leatherstocking region includes the cities of Rome, Utica, and Ithaca. Here the past is kept alive, both intentionally, with many museums, monuments, and historic sites, and inadvertently. From Liverpool to Binghamton, masses of phantoms have been spotted, as well as Men in Black and UFOs.

Ancestors Inn at the Bassett House

Just outside of Syracuse, in the quaint little village of Liverpool, is a large brick Italianate house that has been restored to its original splendor of yesteryear, so well that the previous occupants apparently have returned to dwell among the living. The sixth proprietors, innkeepers Mary and Dan Weidman, believe their historic bed-and-breakfast is haunted by at least a couple friendly spirits—those of its former owners.

The original owners, George and Hannah Bassett, moved into the house upon its completion in 1860; they were among the earliest settlers in the village. George, a prosperous local merchant, passed the large home on to his only son, Henry, when he died. Though Henry had built a smaller, more suitable home for his mother just two doors down, Hannah refused to leave the home she and her husband had put their heart and soul into. She stayed there until the day she died, and some believe that she, along with George, may be there yet.

The Weidmans purchased the Bassett House in 1998, after an exhaustive search for just the right bed-and-breakfast property. As often happens during renovations of haunted abodes, the paranormal activity was stirred up as surely as the sheetrock dust. Tools were moved around by unseen hands, prompting the ambitious new owners to accuse each other of misplacing them. The lights sometimes turned on after the couple had left for the day—even after they went through and thoroughly double-checked that all the lights were off at the time of their departure. It mostly happened in the bedroom believed to have been the Bassetts' bedroom at one time. Sometimes the light in that room would be back on even before Mary reached her car parked in the driveway.

When the inn opened later that year, the Weidmans realized they weren't alone in believing their home was haunted. A couple guests reported seeing a waif of a man sitting in the parlor. The same kindly apparition apparently even sat to join one couple, before getting up to leave. A visiting psychic also told the Weidmans that a benevolent spirit named Tim, who was a servant to the Bassetts in the 1800s, watches over their family and house, still keeping an eye on the property he cared for while alive. For that reason, they affectionately place blame on Tim whenever something doesn't seem quite right.

Mary believes the ghosts are especially attracted to her daughter, Becky, who has a 35-millimeter camera that uses Advantix film. "On two separate occasions," she said "we found unused packages of this film in a little-used cupboard in the public guest area. This cupboard holds books and games and is available to guests but is not a place where someone would store their film for the night. My guess is that one of the ghosts collected the film as a gift for Becky."

She also said that Becky's fiancé, Mark, was "pooh-poohing the whole ghost thing" one night when they were visiting at Christmastime. "Becky had turned on the heat lamps in the bathroom of the room called 'Steve and Elma's Room' to warm it up before taking a shower. Just as Mark was talking, the lamps started flickering on and off. Becky went in to see if maybe she hadn't turned on the switch all the way, but it was okay. She went back out in the room, and the lights flickered again. After that, Mark locked the bedroom door and was a little leery of getting up in the middle of the night."

The Valentine's Room seems to be the most haunted room in the home. Several guests have reported seeing and hearing the doorknob rattle, as if someone were checking to see whether it was locked. Interestingly, Mary had a premonition of the original decor of that room before she ever knew what lay beneath the surface—of the walls, that is. During remodeling, she quickly chose the name and theme for the room and told her husband she envisioned it in opulent red-and-black wallpaper with gold highlights. He reluctantly agreed to it, so they set about removing the old layers of wallpaper before putting up the new. Imagine their surprise when they got to the bottom layer, the original wallpaper, and found that it was exactly the type Mary had envisioned. The same thing happened in another room for which Mary chose the theme. A vision of walls covered with bunches of violets popped into her head, and days later she discovered that, once again, her taste in wallpaper was identical to that of Hannah Bassett!

Besides the Advantix film conundrum, other strange things happen to visitors' cameras. They disappear from obvious places where they have been set and subsequently cannot be found, or if they are found, it's in rooms where the guest had never gone. When visitors are able to get away with their cameras and film intact, there's a chance that some of their pictures won't turn out, unless Mary or Dan happened to be in the photographs when they were taken. So if you're looking for a nice stay in a haunted bed-and-breakfast, book the Valentine's Room at the Ancestors Inn . . . and see what develops.

Belknap's Ghost

Nobody recounts tales of greed and its eternal ramifications quite as memorably as nineteenth-century folklorist Charles M. Skinner. In his 1896 *Myths and Legends of Our Own Land: As to Buried Treasure and Storied Waters, Cliffs, and Mountains,* he shares the misfortune that befell an absentminded farmer:

> On the shore of Oneida Lake is an Indian's grave, where a ball of light [an orb] is wont to swing and dance. A farmer named Belknap dreamed several times of a buried treasure at this point, and he was told, in his vision, that if he would dig there at midnight he could make it his own. He made the attempt, and his pick struck a crock that gave a chink, as of gold. He should, at that moment, have turned around three times, as his dream directed, but he was so excited that he forgot to. A flash of lightning rent the air and stretched him senseless on the grass. When he recovered the crock was gone, the hole filled in, and ever since then the light has hovered about the place. Some say that this is but the will-o'-the-wisp: the soul of a bad fellow who is doomed to wander in desolate regions because, after dying, Peter would not allow him to enter heaven, and the devil would not let him go into the other place, lest he should make the little devils unmanageable; but he is allowed to carry a light in his wanderings.

Syracuse City Hall

As far as haunted landmarks go, the Syracuse City Hall certainly looks the part. The limestone fortress was built in 1892 in a fashion clearly influenced by the archetypal European castle: steeped dormers, stone-barred windows, a triple-arched entrance, turrets of varying sizes, and a striking bell tower that stands twice as high as the rest of the five-story structure. It doesn't take much imagination to conjure up a ghost or two in such a place. But imagination alone can't push buttons to operate the elevator. And imagination alone can't open and close doors when nobody is around and make the sound of footsteps going up and down the corridors of an otherwise empty building. Only a real ghost could accomplish such feats.

At least one longtime employee of City Hall believes the old building is haunted. She has worked in the maintenance department for many years and has seen and heard enough to convince even the toughest skeptics that there are ghosts afoot—or afloat, as the case may be. She has heard the rear elevator operate in the middle of the night when she was the only person on the premises. Other employees have also had strange experiences with the elevators, and technicians were brought in but have been unable to determine why the rear elevator seems to have a mind of its own. Perhaps the electronic push-button elevators that replaced the original pulley-type, hand-operated ones are just too tempting for someone who never experienced such a novel idea while alive. Ghosts do seem to be especially drawn to modern-day fixtures and appliances.

There are a couple theories as to why City Hall might be haunted. Some say that perhaps it's a former prisoner from City Hall's jailhouse days, when prisoners were housed in the basement, which is undoubtedly the most haunted area of the entire building. While down there, many people sense that they are being watched, and some feel cold drafts pass right through them or swirl around them. Others speculate that the ghost is a former mayor who put his job on the line to ensure that the bell in the original City Hall's tower be installed in the new building, whose architect didn't want his contemporary structure ruined by an obsolete old bell. The public was divided on the matter, and the issue may have led to the mayor's defeat in the next election. But he won his battle of the bell. It was placed in the new City Hall's tower and remained there for another fifty years. And the mayor's ghost may remain there to this day.

Cherry Hill

The elegant Cherry Hill estate in Albany, which belonged to the prominent Van Rensselaer family from the late eighteenth century through the mid-twentieth century, was once the scene of a highly publicized crime that resulted in the last public hanging in New York State. It also resulted in a modern-day ghost story.

The Philip Van Rensselaer mansion was built in 1787 at 523½ South Pearl Street. Van Rensselaer's manager, John Whipple, handled all business and financial matters on the impressive nine hundred-acre farm. While Whipple was hard at work, his wife allegedly enjoyed the company of a migrant worker named Jesse Strang. The two collaborated on a plan to murder Whipple so his wife could be with Strang. On May 7, 1827, as the manager sat with Van Rensselaer discussing business, a single shot was fired through a nearby window, killing Whipple instantly. It was determined that Strang had purchased the murder weapon for the sole purpose of shooting Whipple, and he was immediately convicted and sentenced to be hanged. Whipple's wife was sentenced only to jail time, even though she was the mastermind of the crime.

Since that fateful day, nearby residents claim to have seen an apparition on the lower floor and terrace, but nobody knows for certain who it is. It could be any member of the five generations of Van Rensselaers that called the mansion home. It could be Strang, waiting eternally for Whipple's wife to join him, since he had been willing to throw away his own life for the chance to be united with her. Or, perhaps most likely, it's Whipple himself, whose time was cut short so brutally.

Today Cherry Hill is a house-museum with thousands of objects, including manuscripts, textiles, books, and photographs that belonged to the Van Rensselaer family. Author and folklorist Louis C. Jones wrote about the incident in a 1980 book entitled *Murder at Cherry Hill: The Strang-Whipple Case, 1827.* Jones was Director Emeritus of the New York State Historical Association until the time of his death, as well as the co-founder of the New York Folklore Society. He also wrote the 1983 *Things that Go Bump in the Night,* a collection of New York State ghost stories, including one about Cherry Hill, according to the Cherry Hill web site. However, present staff stress that the museum teaches sound history and, while they have publications and tours regarding the murder, there is currently no documentation of any ghost on site.

Cohoes Music Hall

The building that houses the Cohoes Music Hall was built in 1874, with the entire third floor of the massive structure that stands at 58 Remsen Street devoted exclusively to the music hall. Toward the end of the vaudeville era, which had made the hall a prosperous venue, business slowed to the point that the National Bank of Cohoes, owner of the building at the time, closed the theater. It sat vacant and unused for many years, with a roof in dire need of repair. Finally, in 1974, on the one-hundredth anniversary of the theater, the restored music hall, now owned by the city of Cohoes, reopened and was listed on the National Register of Historic Places. Today the Spindle City Historic Society and the Hudson-Mohawk Heritage Area (RiverSpark) Visitor Center call the first floor home.

Apparitions were sighted virtually from the day the theater reopened. Maybe they had been there all along, throughout the deserted first half of the century, but who would have known? By far the most active ghost is that of a woman who often appears in the balcony. Some observers have been close enough to see anger in her eyes. People have described her in so many different ways that it may not be the same ghost each time. Some have reported a woman wearing 1930s clothing; others say she had on a black dress; but most who have seen the filmy apparition say she was a dead ringer for Eva Tanguay, one of vaudeville's biggest names, and the sweetheart of Cohoes for quite some time. Tanguay reached legendary status at Cohoes Music Hall before moving on to Ziegfeld's Follies and eventually taking her famous act on the road. But for all her fame, she died alone and penniless in California in 1947. Her fondness of the music hall and the love interest she once had while there may have been motive enough for her posthumous return.

Cohoes Music Hall may have other ghosts as well. Though it may be Eva who is hanging around the balcony of her beloved theater, who could be causing the elevator to malfunction at the most inopportune times, interrupting the performers and their show? It got so bad on one occasion, the doors opening and closing without any riders, that management had to shut the elevator off. Items that are placed beside the stage just before performances have vanished, and items that are not needed, such as old props used by the likes of Buffalo Bill Cody, Tom Thumb, and Eva Tanguay, have appeared out nowhere. Could it be the work of a former stage manager who died when a sandbag fell on him? Is he still trying to run his stage? An apparition of a man in the aisles and onstage has been reported by several individuals. And a man's disembodied voice has been heard a number of times, but no source for the voice could be found.

Those who study the paranormal know that ghosts can be found anywhere. Wherever man has walked, spirits linger. But there are certain places that seem to have a disproportionate amount of paranormal activity: cemeteries, hospitals, schools, bars, and—you guessed it—theaters.

Devil's Elbow

A dangerous curve in Binghamton called Devil's Elbow, on State Highway 17C three miles west of Owego, was the scene of several fatal automobile accidents in the 1930s. One of the victims apparently haunted the roadside for years, leading to Binghamton's own version of the popular "vanishing hitchhiker" legend.

The story goes that late one evening in October, a man was negotiating the curve during a heavy downpour when he saw a young lady by the side of the road. She wore a white coat and a scarf over her head, and being the gentleman he was, he pulled over and asked her if she needed a lift. She graciously accepted, climbed into the front seat, and asked to be let out at a house just a short distance away. Because she was trembling from the cold, the man chivalrously gave her his jacket to put over her shoulders. Just as he pulled up to the house, the young lady vanished along with his jacket, leaving nothing but a puddle in the seat beside him.

It was impossible; she hadn't even opened the door. Nonetheless, the perplexed fellow was determined to retrieve his jacket. So he walked up to the door of the house the young woman had asked him to bring her to and knocked at the door. An elderly woman answered, and he explained what had happened and asked if the young lady in the white coat was inside with his jacket. The woman then told him that her daughter—the young woman he had described—had died in an accident at Devil's Elbow ten years earlier during a rainstorm, and whenever it rained since then, she tried to come home. Whatever became of the man's jacket is anybody's guess. But others continued to see the lady in white at Devil's Elbow for years.

Forest Park Cemetery

Life magazine once listed Brunswick's Forest Park Cemetery as one of its "Top Ten Most Haunted Places in the United States." This aged and weedy cemetery on Pinewood Avenue was built in 1897 as part of a master plan for two hundred acres of rolling hills and beautiful landscaping—a cemetery the community could be proud of. In the end, it encompassed only twenty-two acres, and it has long been forsaken and vandalized. Had it not been for tales of bleeding statues and crying phantom babies, along with some enduring urban legends and the publicity they brought, it likely would have been completely forgotten, as old cemeteries so often are.

Because of its location adjacent to Pinewood Avenue, locals often refer to the cemetery as Pinewood Cemetery, but its proper name is Forest Park Cemetery. People also call it the Gateway to Hell. The cemetery was built on the site of another small, unknown graveyard, and some speculate that it was an Indian burial ground at one time. Sadly, vandals have decapitated statues, which led to rumors that some of those statues were bleeding from the neck, though there's no proof of that. Many people claim to have heard a baby crying, but others blame the sound on feral cats.

Brunswick also has its own "hitchhiking ghost" legend associated with the cemetery. According to an article in the October 27, 1996, *Troy Record,* a cab driver told a local historian that he had picked up a young girl dressed in party clothes at the Emma Willard School one night. She needed a ride home and asked him to drive up Pinewood Avenue. Just as they neared the cemetery, the girl vanished from the front seat without ever opening the door or even paying the driver.

Another urban legend associated with the cemetery is one often told at slumber parties. Storytellers can make it as gruesome or mild as they want, and they can place it at any location; that's the nature of urban legends. The Forest Park legend, which was also told in the same issue of the *Troy Record,* has a young couple romancing in the solitude of the cemetery in the 1940s or 1950s. The man got out of the vehicle to investigate a strange noise they heard, and the next thing she knew, the young woman—who had been hearing an unusual scraping noise on the hood of the car since shortly after her boyfriend got out—saw police cars approaching. They must have seen the man's body dangling directly over the car, with his feet brushing against the hood as the body swayed, and they knew they had a murder on their hands. The story ends with them telling the horrified woman to run toward them and not look back. If that's not enough to keep you away from Forest Park Cemetery when you're looking for a deserted place to go parking, nothing is.

Griffis Air Force Base Incident

According to an Associated Press story of July 3, 1954, "A jet fighter plane returning from a quick 'scramble' to investigate an unidentified plane, later reported to be 'friendly,' crashed in flames in a crossroads hamlet" the previous day. That was the official spin on a bizarre incident that claimed the lives of four residents of the small town of Walesville, eleven miles southwest of Utica, who were killed by a wayward F-94 Starfire jet. The article went on to explain how two lieutenants—one a radar man and the other a pilot—with the 27th Fighter Interceptor Squadron at Griffis Air Force Base were forced to bail out of their jet when a fire broke out in the cockpit shortly after they scrambled to intercept another flying object in the area. "Scrambling" means to engage in emergency flights. The two were in pursuit of an unidentified flying object, said by some sources to have been "a gleaming disc-shaped machine," over the southern shores of Lake Ontario, where it was being tracked by radar at Griffis AFB in Rome.

As they closed in on their target, their jet was allegedly blasted by heat from either the object they were pursuing or an unknown source. They were forced to bail, and the unpiloted jet slammed into two houses and a car, killing a mother who was making lunch for her children and a family of three in the car.

According to a Griffis AFB public-relations spokesperson, "No information was available on the unidentified plane or where it was located by the jets." Yet she did say that the pilot and radar observer had determined the mysterious plane seen on radar was "friendly" and were headed back to base when the fire broke out in the cockpit. How could they have determined that the object was friendly if they hadn't identified it, as the spokesperson first said?

To this day, the so-called "plane" has never been identified, at least not publicly. A UP release from July 2, 1954, stated that "an Air Force spokesman in Washington said the intercepted plane probably was one that had failed to file a flight plan with the Civil Aeronautics Administration or one that had drifted off its announced flight path." The unexplained fire in the cockpit was brushed off as "merely engine trouble." And all involved in the incident were quickly silenced. Contradictory statements from the Air Force plagued this incident from the start, causing many to wonder what was being covered up.

Landmark Theatre

All historic old theaters should have a "lady in white" in their balconies—a silent and mysterious apparition infusing a sense of awe, if not outright fear, into an already charged atmosphere. The Landmark Theatre at 362 South Salina Street in Syracuse has its own "darling of the balcony," though some would argue that she's anything but darling.

When Thomas Lamb designed the large and lavish theater, originally called Loew's State Theatre, in 1928, he spared no expense on details. His vision was a grandiose venue that would provide its patrons with "the ultimate escape," according to the theater's website—an escape that would take them through the country's good times and bad. And the Landmark Theatre certainly has accomplished that objective, seeing people through World War II and the Great Depression.

Its popularity never waned until the 1950s. By the 1970s, developers wanted to level the building to make way for a new shopping center and parking lot. A group of concerned citizens calling itself SALT, for Syracuse Area Landmark Theatre, began the urgent process of having the property designated a historic landmark. Their efforts were rewarded when the property was placed on the National Register of Historic Places, allowing the group to seek government funding for the restoration of the beloved theater. In 1977, the group bought the theater and began restoring it to its original splendor. And that's when the ghost made her first appearance, probably eager to have the theater returned to its condition of yesteryear—of her time there.

The woman, since dubbed Claire, was most often seen in the balcony, weaving in and out between the aisles or sitting quietly. She wore a long white gown but looked a little fuzzy around the edges. Ushers occasionally approached her to ask her to leave the area, and she gladly complied, quickly vanishing into thin air, much to their astonishment. Some people have also seen a blue orb drifting through different areas of the theater, sometimes along the catwalk, other times on the stairs to the dressing room, and most often along the back side of the auditorium. Though many people still claim to feel mysterious cold spots, hear names whispered by unknown sources, and perceive ethereal voices in the darkness of an empty room, the management doesn't necessarily believe the place is haunted—at least not anymore. No visions of the lady in white have been reported in many years, but people still feel electricity in the air when they enter the building—whether it's because the air is supernaturally stimulated or because of the expectation of possibly experiencing something paranormal. Or maybe it's simply the anticipation of seeing the famous Syracuse Symphony perform live.

Men in Black

According to Timothy Green Beckley's 1990 book *The UFO Silencers*, Men in Black may have intermingled with the general population of Scotia for a four-year period, beginning in 1967. During that time, residents of Scotia reported UFO sightings along the Mohawk River, and people who saw the unidentified flying objects experienced a broad range of paranormal phenomena, including encounters with possible Men in Black.

It all started when a woman, identified only as Peggy G., was walking a friend to her car at about 11 P.M. one night in April 1967. The two women stopped to look at a bright star that had caught their attention, when it suddenly shot forward and stopped just short of them. The hovering object then spit a baseball-size projectile out over their heads and into the woods across the street. Six weeks later, more UFOs were spotted around town. At the same time, residents were reporting an unusually high number of missing pets, one lady even claiming her dog was kidnapped by "little men."

As if the bizarre encounter with a UFO weren't enough for Peggy, the young woman was also dealing with other paranormal phenomena at her own house. She had begun to see apparitions of a man, objects were moving by themselves, and her cat was constantly agitated by something Peggy couldn't see. When she took on a new job over the Christmas holidays, an employee who was hired as a guard told her at lunch one day that he was a member of a secret organization working on Earth. Another employee within earshot heard the conversation and whispered under his breath that the guy was crazy. The guard became inflamed and told the employee he would turn himself into the most horrible thing the man had ever seen if he didn't get away from him and forget what he had heard. Angry rays of light shot from the guard's eyes directly at the outspoken employee. A few days later, the guard left his job and was never seen again.

A couple months later, two young men spotted a flying saucer in the middle of the frozen Mohawk River, along with what looked like a person dressed in white right beside the object. The next morning, a teenage boy was found dead at the same location, his body frozen in the ice. The police said it appeared, from his tracks, as if he had been running and then was pulled upward, because of the way the last few footprints dragged. The boy's cause of death was officially reported as "due to exposure." Local residents weren't buying it; too many unexplained things had been happening. A local UFO organization staked out the riverside for several nights in a row to see if they could find any clues to the real cause of death. They were rewarded by a reddish oval object that hovered nearby one night and had a particular blinking pattern that lasted for several minutes. When a plane went by, the object disappeared.

A few days later, a UFO researcher's husband was sitting in a local coffee shop when a strange man sat down beside him and began discussing the events surrounding the most recent UFO sighting. He knew information that wasn't available to anyone outside of the immediate group of researchers. Before he got up to leave, he said dryly, "People who look for UFOs should be very, very careful." The man looked, talked, and acted like one of the typical Men in Black, and this was their proverbial threat. Every member of the group that had been scanning the river's edge for clues to the boy's death was followed at one time or another by a light blue Lincoln for the next three weeks. Sometimes the Lincoln parked on the street outside their homes for hours. Eventually everything settled down . . . the Men in Black left, the UFOs left, and the accompanying paranormal activity ceased. Apparently, the mission—whatever it was—had been accomplished.

Mosqueto, the Lake Onondaga Monster

Charles M. Skinner was an American folklorist and the author of the Myths and Legends of Our Own Land series in the late 1890s and *American Myths and Legends* in 1903; for those, he became a legend of sorts himself. In the 1896 *Myths and Legends of Our Own Land: The Hudson and Its Hills*, Skinner offers his spin on the fascinating Native American legend of Mosqueto, the giant, man-eating mosquito of Onondaga Lake, said to be the ancestor of today's local bloodthirsty insects: "They have some pretty big mosquitoes in New Jersey and on Long Island, but, if report of their ancestry is true, they have degenerated in size and voracity; for the grandfather of all mosquitoes used to live in the neighborhood of Fort Onondaga, New York, and sallying out whenever he was hungry, would eat an Indian or two and pick his teeth with their ribs." The Indians were helpless against the creature, but the "Holder of the Heavens" came to their aid and killed it by the shores of Onondaga.

"As its blood poured upon the earth," the story goes, "it became small mosquitoes that gathered about the Holder of the Heavens and stung him so sorely that he half repented the service that he had done to men." The Tuscaroras have a stone on their reservation marking this event, showing where the Holder of the Heavens rested during the chase. South of Syracuse, says Skinner, his tracks were seen alternating with the mosquito's footprints, "which were shaped like those of a bird, and twenty inches long! At Brighton, New York, where these marks appeared, they were reverentially renewed by the Indians for many years."

New York State Capitol Building

Every town seems to have its haunted house on the hill, and Albany is no different. It just does things in a much bigger way, which one might expect of a state capital. Albany's version sits atop State Street Hill: the imposing New York State Capitol building. It's not a house, per se, but a certain ghost is believed to have taken up eternal residence there. Is it George, the unknown janitor, as many have

dubbed the innocuous resident ghost? Or is it a night watchman who died in the fire that nearly consumed the building's library in 1911, as one psychic suggested? People have heard keys jangling where nobody is standing, as well as doorknobs rattling, and found doors open for no reason. Who but a watchman or janitor would be a more likely perpetrator of such ghostly antics as those that have plagued the Assembly Chamber for decades?

The elaborately designed State Capitol was considered a modern marvel of nineteenth-century architecture when it was completed in 1899, after more than twenty-five years and at a cost of $25 million. Calamity struck in 1911, when a fire engulfed the State Library, destroying 750,000 historic books and manuscripts. Firefighters fought for many hours to save the structure and its contents, but nobody was able to save Sam Abbott, the night watchman on duty that fateful night.

In the years since that devastating fire, employees and visitors have heard muted voices after hours, and many swear that they've seen inexplicable shadows moving through the fifth-floor chambers. One employee saw a grayish blur approaching her and felt its chill pass right through her body, before it raced past another employee so rapidly that the woman's skirt was lifted by the breeze, according to an account described in Arthur Myers's 1986 book, *The Ghostly Register*. Perhaps the night watchman continues to repeat his last frantic sprint from room to room amid the flames of the devastating fire that claimed his life so many years ago.

The Station Restaurant and Sleeping Cars

The ghosts of two women dressed in Victorian-style clothing at the Station Restaurant are so well known that a special chair has been placed at the very spot where they've been seen standing, as if waiting on the platform for their train to arrive. Customers can take souvenir photographs, and ghost enthusiasts can take pictures—or have their pictures taken—and perhaps be lucky enough to capture the spirits' essence on film.

In 1965, Joe Ciaschi purchased the Lehigh Valley Railroad Station building, originally built in 1885 at 806 West Buffalo Street, and turned it into a restaurant, cleverly enclosing the platform area and using the authentic dining cars on their actual tracks. Under the management of Joe's son, Terry, three of the dining cars were converted into luxurious private sleeping cars several years ago, providing unique accommodations for weary travelers. One of those sleeping cars—the Red Sleeper—may even offer a little something extra for especially brave adventurers, although my own stay in the sleeper was paranormally uneventful. Terry's wife said she passes through the Red Sleeper especially quickly when she has to go from car to car, because she feels so uncomfortable in it, as if she's not alone. It's the only one of the three lavish sleeping cars that she has ever felt anxious in. She's well versed in the stories of an apparition of a woman wearing 1800s-style clothing being seen in the big old mirror that was once in that room. Now the mirror is between the dining room and bar area, and a waitress at the restaurant said she has seen unusual shadows in it, even from the other side of the room, when she's the only person around.

Terry didn't really believe much in the ghost story hype associated with the place, until he had his own inexplicable incident. He has always propped open the swinging door in the kitchen with a wedge that stays so securely in place that it takes a bit of effort to remove it. The day after he dismissed the notion of the place being haunted to his employees, he found the wedge knocked out, even though he was the only one in the building at the time. Sometimes it takes a little scare to put people on the right "track."

Western New York

WESTERN NEW YORK IS GENERALLY DIVIDED INTO THREE DISTINCT regions: Finger Lakes, Greater Niagara, and Chautauqua-Allegheny. When the ice-age glaciers raked through the rich, friable soil of the Finger Lakes region, they created eleven lakes, nearly a thousand waterfalls, and hundreds of deep valleys and gorges, including one dubbed the "Grand Canyon of the East," which stretches from the Finger Lakes region into the Greater Niagara region. Today these lakes are a favorite getaway spot for wine lovers, with many vineyards and wineries located along the world-famous Seneca Lake Wine Trail, including the newest addition, the winery of Geneva's haunted Belhurst Castle. But you don't have to drink a lot of wine to see ghosts in this region.

The Greater Niagara region is most famous for its majestic Niagara Falls. But there are plenty of other things to get excited about nearby. For daring types, a visit to Devil's Hole, often called the unluckiest place in New York, may satisfy their appetite for risk-taking; others may be satiated by historic sites like Old Fort Niagara, a pre-Revolutionary fort where spirits from the period are said to dwell. Still hungry? Not long ago you could get a burger and fries (and maybe a ghost) at the Frontier House, then a McDonald's Restaurant, in Lewiston. Had enough? If that weren't enough, you could head to the Holiday Inn on Grand Island to see if you could hear little Tanya, the ghost, skipping up and down the hallway outside your door. For thrills and chills, few places can compete with Greater Niagara.

The Chautauqua-Allegheny region is in the southwestern corner of the state, bordering Lake Erie and Pennsylvania. Its Allegheny State Park is the largest in New York, making this region prime territory for outdoor activities such as camping, fishing, canoeing, and swimming. Of the three regions that make up Western New York, Chautauqua-Allegheny is by far the most rural and unhurried—and the least haunted, but that doesn't mean you don't have to watch your back. There may not be as many ghosts, but some of the paranormal stories coming out of this region are *X-Files* storyline material: the Cherry Creek UFO incident; the creature from Black Creek, best described as an abominable snowman or albino Bigfoot; and the mysterious, isolated Zoar Valley race of Clawfoot people, who intentionally eradicated their entire population.

Belhurst Castle

The Seneca Indians were the first known people to inhabit the land on which Belhurst Castle now sits, overlooking the lake named in that tribe's honor. The property, located at 4069 Route 14 South in Geneva, was originally part of the commonwealth of Massachusetts. In the 1800s, it served as commercial property for a glass-manufacturing company—the first glass company west of Albany. Englishman Joseph Fellows had the first residence constructed on the land in 1820 and dubbed it the Hermitage. However, William Henry Bucke, better known as Bucke Hall, was the first person to actually live at the Hermitage. Hall fled to the United States from London, where he had been the treasurer of a prominent theater, to avoid capture and prosecution for embezzling theater funds. His tainted past wasn't uncovered until his death by blood poisoning in 1836. The property then passed through the hands of several owners, before finally being obtained in 1885 by Carrie Harron. This ambitious society woman hired fifty men to tear down the Hermitage and raise Belhurst Castle, which they did in just four years' time. During construction, one employee died from a fall off the tower, and another went insane while roofing.

From the 1930s to the 1970s, Belhurst flourished as an outstanding restaurant and casino. In 1975, it was converted into a lodging establishment, and today, under the ownership of the Duane Reeder family, it boasts a four-diamond rating. Belhurst, which means "beautiful forest," was voted one of the most romantic places in New York State and is on the National Register of Historic Places. Like many places with that honor, it also has some ghost stories attached, including my own.

A few have reported hearing the faint sounds of a baby crying and a woman singing lullabies in the Billiard Room, as well as in other rooms throughout the castle. An apparition of a man in the men's room has been reported sporadically. Many believe it's the spirit of an earlier owner's friend who died of a heart attack during the 1930s, but perhaps it's the ghost of Bucke Hall or the opera singer's unfortunate lover, who is rumored to have perished along with the singer when a tunnel in which they were hiding on the grounds collapsed.

The most enduring story involves the White Lady, believed to be the spirit of an opera singer who fled with her lover from Spain to Geneva to avoid scandal. An apparition of a woman in white has been spotted drifting along the shore of the lake on the castle's front lawn, and a similar apparition has been seen on the private balcony of the Billiard Room, one of fourteen elaborate guest rooms. When I stayed in that room, I was startled to hear eight distinct taps on the balcony window directly above my headboard shortly after midnight. I looked up but saw nothing moving outside the window where the sound came from. Though I had hoped for paranormal activity that night, I hadn't really expected it. And frankly, my reaction to the puzzling incident disappointed me, as it seemed unbecoming of an author of my genre. On shaky legs, I hobbled over to the lamp and spent the rest of the night with the light on and one eye open. So much for the brave ghost-story seeker!

Cherry Creek Incident

Nobody knows why the summer of 1965 was such an active period for UFOs over Western New York, though conspiracy theorists have hinted that it was a prelude to the Great Northeast Power Blackout that November, when widespread UFO sightings occurred at the outset of the massive outages, giving rise to speculation that they were somehow responsible. At any rate, the most famous sighting that summer took place on a dairy farm in Cherry Creek.

It was about 8:20 P.M. on August 19. Sixteen-year-old Harold was running the milking machine when a commotion started outside. A young Holstein bull tied to a steel bar by its nose on the outside of the barn was making a hideous noise, the likes of which Harold had never before heard come from an animal, and he'd heard a lot of animal noises while living on a farm. At the same time that the bull was bellowing, the radio—which had been crisp and clear an instant before—became garbled with static and white noise, and the milking-machine motor died. Harold could see the bull trying to break loose, but then his attention was quickly drawn toward an elliptical object about fifty feet long hovering just over the nearby tree line. When the UFO was about ten feet off the ground, Harold was close enough to see what looked like red vapor shooting out from beneath it. At first the only noise it made was a strange beeping sound, but when it rose moments later behind the clouds, it became so loud that the young man compared the blare to a sonic boom in intensity.

He ran into the house, where his mother was trying to tune her radio back in, and got his brother, Robert, to run outside with him. By then the object had reappeared from behind the clouds and was once again hovering over the tree line. As it rose a second time, it left a trail of red mist in its wake and gave the clouds it hid behind a greenish glow. Nobody else saw the UFO at that moment; however, a short time later, a neighbor ran into the house and said the spacecraft was back. This time, everyone in the house and on the farm saw it except Harold's mother.

When police officers arrived at the scene, they recognized the distinct odor of phosphine at the location where the object had been seen, and found an unidentified purple substance with an oily smell in an area where the grass was singed. Samples of the substance, as well as some of the grass and soil, were taken by the Niagara Falls Air Force Base. Results of the chemical analyses were never made public, perhaps because the strange elements were like nothing known to mankind. The investigation into the sighting was so convincing that the incident was awarded the coveted "unexplained" status by the U.S. Air Force's Project Blue Book.

Devil's Hole

Devil's Hole, at Niagara Falls, is thought to be the unluckiest place in New York State, a place where tragedy begets tragedy. That designation of ill fate puts this cave in the running for the most haunted location in Western New York, for many have heard moans and ethereal screams emanating from within. Niagara Falls, being the powerful force that it is, has played host to innumerable murders, suicides, and accidents for as long as man has inhabited the region. And all of that misfortune seems to have drifted about three miles downriver from the falls and settled at the twenty-foot-deep cave and chasm the early Senecas called Devil's Hole.

The Indians believed the cave was the home of a demonlike snake they called the Evil One for its propensity to orchestrate all that was malevolent. And no wonder. Some of their tribe entered and never came out. Others returned with their hair—dark just the day before—having turned solid white from the terror of whatever they had encountered, which they couldn't describe because they had lost their minds inside the cave.

So frightened were Indians of the Evil One that in 1687, the Iroquois tried to warn the early French explorer Sieur de La Salle to avoid that area. He didn't listen and shortly thereafter was murdered by his own men. Then in 1763, during a conflict known as the Conspiracy of Pontiac, the Senecas ambushed, scalped, and mutilated a group of eighty British troops and threw the men and their horses into Devil's Hole. The incident became known as the Devil's Hole Massacre. The next prominent incident related to Devil's Hole occurred in 1901, when President William McKinley was assassinated just hours after passing by the cave on the Great Gorge Trolley. Sixteen years later, the Great Gorge Trolley lost one of its cars at the very moment it was passing by Devil's Hole, sending fifty passengers into the murderous mouth of the beast.

According to Dennis William Hauck's *Haunted Places: The National Directory* (2002), someone dies by falling or drowning near the cave almost every year. Though there hasn't been a large-scale loss of life in quite some time, who knows when the Evil One will once again look for more than a mere morsel? If you're already prone to bad luck, you may not be wise to tempt fate by visiting a place said to be "cursed with an aura of sheer bad luck." But if you feel you must visit Devil's Hole just to say you survived it, it's located off NY Route 104 at Devil's Hole Park and is open to the public. Just don't say you weren't warned.

Fort Niagara

Western New York plays host to many ghosts, but ranking right up there at the top of its list of most-haunted sites is Fort Niagara, home of Henri the Headless and a horrible hobgoblin. Fort Niagara is one of the country's oldest forts, its first structure, the French Castle, constructed in 1726. Overlooking the Niagara River in Youngstown, the fort was a highly desired strategic location, taken over alternately by France, Canada, the United States, and Great Britain—because whoever had control over it also controlled access to the Great Lakes and the passage west. Before its designation as Fort Niagara, the site was a trading post established by French explorer Sieur de La Salle for trade with the Iroquois Nation. And before that, the ancient Native Americans had built fort after fort at the same location. With all that history under its belt, the fort was destined to become ghost-infested one day.

That day came the moment Henri LeClerc's head hit the floor. The legend of LeClerc was first told in a small publication written in 1839 by Samuel De Veaux. At the Battle of Fort Niagara in 1759, LeClerc agreed to a swordfight with another Frenchman over the affections of an Indian maiden. When Henri, the man the maiden really wanted, lost his balance, his opponent wasted no time decapitating him. LeClerc's head and body were separated, one thrown into a well and the other into the river, though various accounts differ on which part went where. Henri's headless ghost was later seen wandering around the French Castle, dazed and confused; not surprising, since he was missing his thinking parts.

Even before De Veaux wrote about the ghost of Henri LeClerc, paranormal activity had been reported on the fort grounds. In the graveyard in 1815, someone reportedly saw a hobgoblin, an ugly, frightening little goblin or elf that harasses the living. Others claim to have seen it over the years in the cemetery and the dreaded dungeon of the mess-house. According to Esther Singleton's *Historic Landmarks of America* (1907):

The dungeon of the mess-house, called the black hole, was a strong, dark, and dismal place; and in one corner of the room was fixed the apparatus for strangling such unhappy wretches as fell under the displeasure of the despotic rulers of those days. The walls of this dungeon, from top to bottom, had engraved upon them French names, and mementos in that language. That the prisoners were no common persons was clear, as the letters and emblems were chiseled out in good style. In June 1812, when an attack was momentarily expected upon the fort by a superior British force, a merchant, resident at Fort Niagara, deposited some valuable articles in this dungeon. He took occasion, one night, to visit it with a light; he examined the walls, and there, among hundreds of French names, he saw his own family name engraved, in large letters!

Needless to say, he never returned for clarification.

Supernatural activity today—as reported by staff and visitors and confirmed by a multitude of paranormal investigators—includes creaking doors and floorboards, disembodied voices and footsteps, flimsy apparitions, dark moving shadows unassociated with any living being and captured on video, dancing lights, shuffled papers, muffled battle sounds, moving chairs and dishes, and strange dreams. It sounds like so much, and yet, if you put it into perspective, recalling that death and mayhem presided over the land at that spot since the first Native American fort in 106 A.D., things could—and probably should—be a lot worse, supernaturally speaking.

Holiday Inn

Probably the most famous hotel ghost in New York State is Tanya, a little girl who has been haunting the Holiday Inn Grand Island Resort and Conference Center at 100 Whitehaven Road on Grand Island for years. Allegedly, a young girl died in a fire that destroyed a house that once sat on the very foundation of the hotel, and now her playful spirit runs about looking for playmates. Even though no records have been found that would support the claim of a girl who died in a fire, it seems that the spirit of a girl wearing an old-fashioned white nightgown roams the halls, whoever she may be.

Employees and guests alike have reported apparitions of a little girl, between five and ten years old, skipping down the hallways, bouncing balls, and jumping on beds. She has even been seen on the grounds, frolicking in the yard, before disappearing around a corner of the building and into thin air. As with most children that age, she never slows down, and sightings of her continue persistently. Tanya's favorite area seems to be the fourth floor, and some guests also have seen another spirit in that area—that of a tall, sinister-looking man who stands beside beds gazing down at guests. Whether he has any connection to Tanya is anyone's guess, since no one knows the little girl's history.

Tanya's hair is consistently said to be long and wild. Even when she isn't seen, she is often heard—perhaps every night by someone, somewhere in the resort, who thinks the pitter-patter of little feet running up and down the corridors are from an inattentive parent's unruly child, completely unaware of Tanya, the playful and friendly ghost.

If they were to look out into the hallways, as one woman I spoke to did, they would most likely continue to hear the footsteps, and they might even feel a slight breeze brush past them—but there would be no child in sight. I leave it to you, the curious reader and adventurous traveler, to put this theory to the test on your next visit to Holiday Inn Grand Island Resort and Conference Center.

McDonald's Frontier House

The now-vacant McDonald's restaurant in Lewiston was in one of the oldest buildings in the Western New York region, formerly known as Frontier House. Many famous personages, including Prince Edward of Wales, James Fenimore Cooper, and President William McKinley, stopped there in its earliest days as a stagecoach stop. And it was quite haunted.

The Frontier House was built in 1824 as the final stop on the Barton Stage Line. Even in those first years as a hotel, employees believed it was haunted, saying that doors opened and closed on their own. Over the years, the paranormal occurrences increased and became more varied. For a time, when it was still a stagecoach stop, the building was used as a Masonic meeting lodge. William Morgan was an outspoken anti-Mason, who became famous for threatening to release an exposé about the covert practices of the Freemasons. Shortly after he made the threat, he mysteriously disappeared. His body has never been found, but many believed for a time that his skeleton would be found somewhere in the walls or basement of the Frontier House. During renovations in the 1960s, no such discovery was made, so he may not be the person who haunted the Frontier House, but clearly someone did.

In 1977, the Frontier House was converted into a McDonald's restaurant. During renovations, tools and equipment disappeared, as often happens in haunted places that are undergoing remodeling. Doors and windows opened and closed inexplicably, even when the building was empty. Strange sounds were often heard. One cleaning lady saw apparitions, such as the ghost of a personable old man in the pantry, more than once. And a former manager claimed to see a silhouette of someone in the bathroom as he showered in the otherwise empty building one night. At least one employee quit shortly after being hired because of something supernatural that he experienced.

The building, owned by Hastings Lewiston, Inc., was vacated on December 12, 2004.

Seneca Falls Historical Society

They say that historic places have a higher proportion of ghosts compared with average, run-of-the-mill buildings. Well, few places could be more historic than a 150-year-old building that houses a historical society, a museum, and a library; and there's nothing like a ghost story or two thrown into the pot to really keep the history interesting. The Seneca Falls Historical Society took up residence in the three-story, twenty-three-room Victorian mansion at 55 Cayuga Street in 1961. The first floor depicts a wealthy family home circa 1890. Apparently, the restoration of the home was so true to life that some of those present during the Victorian era have no inclination of moving on, or out.

There's virtually no denying that it is a haunted environment, though the museum staff stress that theirs is a *friendly* haunted environment. The Beckers were the first to report inexplicable incidents taking place in the circa-1855 home built by Edward Mynderse. They moved into it in 1890, after the widow, Ellen Partridge, had completely renovated the two-story, brick Italianate home into a twenty-three-room Victorian mansion. The museum's education director, Frances T. Barbieri quipped that perhaps Edward "didn't like the change, so he haunts the house to make sure no other tragic changes fall upon it." The Becker family kept the home until the last child, Florence Becker, sold it to the Historical Society in 1961, ghosts and all. Furniture got moved around somehow, clocks stopped ticking, pictures were turned around to face the walls, disturbing noises were heard, and doors opened and closed—and locked and unlocked—by themselves, often leaving the Beckers out in the cold, so to speak.

Since the historical society took over the home, many more unexplained incidents have occurred there. For one thing, the doors are sometimes found locked from the inside by either the hooks or latches, just as they were for the Beckers. One stubborn closet door locks itself, even though there is no lock on it. Historical society staff have heard what sounds like a young girl sobbing on the back steps to the building, but no source for the sound has ever been found. Workers installing a heater in the basement complained about being hounded by a silent and solemn woman in a gray uniform, who stared at them intently as they went about their business. One of the men who saw the woman later noticed her likeness in a Becker family portrait on Barbieri's desk: It was the family maid, Mary Merrigan.

Mary Merrigan features prominently in the ghost stories associated with the house. It seems she appeared in apparitional form to the Becker family shortly after she died. She had been loyal to the Beckers for many years, but eventually she suffered severe dementia and had to be admitted to the Willard State Hospital. On the night she died, she appeared in the Becker family living room wearing her gray work uniform. They assumed she had left the hospital without permission, and since it was late in the evening, they sent her up to her room on the third floor, planning to wake her in the morning and return her to the hospital. The next morning, they found her missing and shortly thereafter received a phone call from the hospital saying she had passed away the night before—at precisely the moment she appeared in their living room. She had come to say good-bye to the dear family she had served so well. And she may still linger yet.

According to Susan Smitten's *Ghost Stories of New York State* (2004), the brother of a historical society employee once made a tape recording in Mary's third-floor room while being given a tour and history of the home. When playing back the tape later, an unidentified female voice in the room could be heard saying, "Excuse me. You hit me." The words were not said by one of the two individuals present in the room at that time, and the mysterious voice sounds cultured, as if from another era. What a fascinating addition to the historical society's collection of authentic items from the past!

The Abominable Snowman

According to author and paranormal researcher Mason Winfield, something strange was seen in the town of Black Creek in Allegany County in the mid-1970s. He dubbed it the "Black Creek Whodat," because nobody knows for sure just what it was. The best eyewitness accounts reported a large, light-colored humanoid creature. Those who got close enough or followed its trail were treated to a very fetid odor that apparently wafted off the beast in its wake.

The first incident, according to Winfield's 2001 book, *Spirits of the Great Hill,* happened in 1973. A handful of high school students from the town of Cuba were camping in a cabin built out in the open and heard strange noises, like someone running around the cabin to purposely scare them. Dogs apparently chased whatever it was but never caught up, as far as anyone knows. In 1975, a camper took a walk late one evening and was terrified to look up at a "humanoid, big, and white" critter. They looked at each other— man and beast—and each promptly tore off in the opposite direction. The camper later said the white beast ran at a superhuman speed. The man's friends thought his tears were fake and he was just trying to scare them, but he wasted no time heading home, leaving his skeptical friends behind at the campsite laughing. They continued laughing even when they heard someone banging on the cabin and making the walls shake, figuring their friend was really laying it on heavy. But the next day, they found dents in the outside walls of the cabin and discovered that their friend really had gone home and hadn't been back to the cabin at all.

Run-ins with the white creature continued for another year, with many people claiming to see "big white things" in the woods and swamp. Locals living near the swamp began to feel a bit nervous, as if they were being watched by the creature whenever they were

outside. Strange lights and noises emanated from the swamp, where the townspeople believed the creature hid, but it was so dense that it was difficult for hunters to navigate it thoroughly. Then there were the reports of terrorized livestock in Black Creek, at the peak of Whodat sightings. And no wonder the cows were traumatized—one of their own was found mutilated outside of one farmer's barn, and the only clue left behind as to the culprit was a putrid, skunk-like smell. But a skunk couldn't have been responsible for that kind of carnage.

The last sighting of what may have been an albino Bigfoot, among other theories, was in 1976, when two men sleeping in a pickup truck were awakened by footsteps circling their vehicle. Then a nearby resident opened a door to let their dog out, and the men saw the creature, which Winfield described as an apparition outracing the dog to the woods. The creature, which reminds me of the Abominable Snowman of Rudolph the Red-nosed Reindeer fame, was never seen again. Incidentally, Bigfoot, or the Yeti, as some call it, is also referred to as the Abominable Snowman some areas.

The Clawfoot People

Legends abound in the rugged wilds of Western New York, but one of the most fascinating I've ever heard is about a population of clawfooted people that wiped itself off the face of the earth—on purpose. The following legend is based on actual events, so I'll give you the original legend, included by folklorist Charles M. Skinner in his 1896 *Myths and Legends of Our Own Land: The Hudson and Its Hills,* as well as the modern-day explanation.

> The valley of Zoar, in Western New York, is so surrounded by hills that its discoverers—a religious people who gave it a name from Scripture said, "This is Zoar; it is impregnable. From here we will never go."
>
> Among the early settlers here were people of a family named Wright, whose house became a sort of inn for the infrequent traveler, inasmuch as they were not troubled with piety and had no scruples against the selling of drink and the playing of cards at late hours. A peddler passed through the valley on his way to Buffalo and stopped at the Wright house for a lodging, but before he went to bed, he incautiously showed a number of golden trinkets

from his pack and drew a considerable quantity of money out of his pocket when he paid the fee for his lodging. Hardly had he fallen asleep before his greedy hosts were in the room, searching for his money. Their lack of caution caused him to awake, and as he found them rifling his pockets and his pack, he sprang up and showed fight.

A blow sent him to the bottom of the stairs, where his attempt to escape was intercepted, and the family closed around him and bound his arms and legs. They showed him the money they had taken and asked where he had concealed the rest. He vowed that it was all he had. They insisted that he had more, and seizing a knife from the table, the elder Wright slashed off one of his toes "to make him confess." No result came from this, and six toes were cut off—three from each foot. Then, in disgust, the unhappy peddler was knocked on the head and flung through a trap door into a shallow cellar. Presently, he arose and tried to draw himself out, but with hatchet and knife, they chopped away his fingers and he fell back. Even the women shared in this work and leaned forward to gaze into the cellar to see if he might yet be dead. While listening, they heard the man invoke the curse of Heaven on them: he asked that they should wear the mark of crime even to the fourth generation, by coming into the world deformed and mutilated as he was then. And it was so. The next child born in that house had round, hoof-like feet, with only two toes, and hands that tapered from the wrist into a single long finger. And in time, there were twenty people so deformed in the valley: The "crab-clawed Zoarites," they were called.

Interestingly, at least one other itinerant salesman named T. Dutton is known to have met a suspicious fate in Zoar Valley, and his burial stone still stands today, though broken in half—next to the foundation of a large farm from the early 1800s. According to a report by the Paranormal and Ghost Society, the man found his way to an early settlement in Zoar Valley in 1826. Shortly after his arrival, he was reported missing, but eventually his body was found. It could never be proven that he was murdered; however, all of his valuables were missing, so it's a distinct possibility he was slaughtered and robbed. His body was cremated on a stone slab, and there allegedly was a carnival in the poor man's name each year. Why the village would celebrate the man's untimely demise is unclear . . . and kind of creepy. But then, a lot of the history of Zoar Valley is creepy. No wonder people believe Zoar Valley is haunted. Why wouldn't it be? Two traveling salesmen murdered in the 1800s—and at least two civilizations vanishing (besides the Clan of the Clawfooted, an extinct civilization predated the first known people who settled there, as evidenced by the pattern and type of vegetation). Much suffering and death have left their impression in the valley.

But here is the *real* story of the Clawfoot People—or at least a more plausible explanation of what happened in Zoar. According to an article from an unknown newspaper, an English prostitute settled in the remote town of Zoar Valley in the early 1800s. The woman suffered from syphilis, a condition related to clawfoot. Her two hundred descendants became carriers of the disfiguring genetic condition or a condition whose range of symptoms included clawfoot.

Clawfoot, or *pes cavus,* is a hereditary condition that presents as a deformity of the foot marked by very high arches and elongated toes. Claw toe is a deformity of the foot in which the toes point downward and there is a high arch, making the foot appear claw-like. It, too, can be present from birth, developing as a consequence of certain genetic disorders. Clawfoot and claw toe, even if not associated with any other underlying diseases, are very painful and deforming conditions; however, they can be easily treated by medical and surgical means today.

All of the males of the Clawfoot People save one suffered from a horrible, life-shortening disease, through no fault of their own, and were shunned by society. The sole male offspring who showed no sign of disease went on to marry a young lady outside the clan, but he never told her of his family's plight. When their first child, a son, was born, he had the clawfoot syndrome. The woman, upon finally hearing her husband confess, ran out of the hospital, abandoning both husband and son.

In the 1920s, the clan of the cursed could stand it no longer, and they unanimously agreed to a secret pact never again to marry or raise families. It was the only way to prevent the disease from being passed on to future generations. They all grew old and eventually died, and today not a single fertile person remains from that family tree—the lineage has been completely obliterated.

The Medina Crop Circles

Ever since the motion picture *Signs*, starring Mel Gibson, came out, everybody knows what crop circles are, and they know that such vegetative anomalies are often associated with UFO sightings. Most New Yorkers, however, are probably unaware that we even have the occasional crop circle in our own state. In 1991, a twenty-foot-wide crop circle was discovered in a wheat field in Medina, Orleans County. To this date, after extensive investigations and testing, nobody has been able to explain what caused it.

Todd Roberts discovered the unusual crop formation in his wheat field on the corner of Salt Works Road and Maple Ridge Road on July 5, 1991. Word quickly spread to the news media and the general public, but before the masses could converge on the poor man's farm, the chairman of the Ultimate Frontiers Organization (UFO), Daryl Hardes, visited the Roberts farm and began a thorough investigation. According to Mason Winfield's 2001 book, *Spirits of the Great Hill*, Hardes described the scene as follows: "Layers of grain laid down in different directions, several deep, without breaking the stalks. They looked like they had grown with a 90-degree bend to lie on the ground. Soil taken from it tested 100 percent sterile, while it was normal outside the circle. That couldn't have been done with ropes and boards." Besides the inexplicable lie of the wheat, the crop was also somewhat discolored.

A scientific investigator of the crop circle phenomenon, found during experimentation that she could replicate the behavior of the seeds of the crop of known circle formations (which did not look like regular seeds, nor did they grow the same) by heating them at a very rapid rate, no longer than thirty seconds. She noted the seeds of the Medina crop as a prime example and said that when scanned under an electron microscope, she "found unusual crystals, like seeds heated by microwave." What could possibly heat the ground so rapidly, and in a perfectly circular shape, producing the peculiar curve in the growth of the crop? Certainly nothing at Roberts's disposal—and quite possibly nothing of this earth.

Before the 1980s, few people were aware of the predominance of crop formations through the world. Years ago, if people heard of them at all, they were considered an ancient mystery. But the past twenty-five years have seen an increasing number of formations, which are becoming ever more elaborate, especially in England. Our own coun-try has been blessed by about fifty crop circles that could not be proven as hoaxes. Four of those were in the Medina area, not far from the most prominent one at the Roberts farm. There are really not as many theories as one might expect about what could cause crop circles, especially the intricately designed ones. How could any known atmospheric phenomenon design such complex patterns in such a small area? Some believe all crop circles are hoaxes by people seeking the public spotlight. But that's not the case in Medina, as Roberts and his wife didn't want attention at all. In fact, they said from the start that their strange field impression was no crop circle, regardless of what others who might know better said.

Most people who study crop circles believe there is a UFO con-nection, thinking that perhaps extraterrestrials are trying to leave us coded messages in the symbolic formations they leave in our fields. In fact, many times UFOs are reported simultaneously with crop circle reports. The evening before the Medina crop circle was discovered, one of the Robertses' neighbors saw strange lights in the air. It would be the perfect explanation, wouldn't it? UFOs are often reported as being round—and what do you know, so are crop circles. UFOs tend to have all kinds of superpowers, so they could probably superheat a freshly seeded wheat field in thirty seconds or less, and in a very precise manner. And if that's not enough to convince the skeptics, who other than aliens would have an under-standable reason to leave symbolic messages all over the world's fields—designs that can only be fully seen and appreciated from an aerial point of view? It's enough to make you want to watch *Signs* again, isn't it?

USS The Sullivans

If ever there was a series of unfortunate events that would culmi-nate in an astronomically implausible tragedy, it was when the Sullivan brothers—Albert, Francis, George, Joseph, and Madison—bravely joined the U.S. Navy in 1942. It seems that the young men were so certain that they would be invincible by sticking together during battle that even now they continue to carry on as if alive on a destroyer-turned-museum named in their honor—sixty-two years after they were killed in World War II.

When the brothers enlisted, they did so under one condition: that they would be allowed to serve on the same ship. For some reason, Navy policy against multiple family members serving together was ignored, and all the brothers were permitted to serve aboard the USS *Juneau*. On November 13, 1942—Friday the thirteenth—during a battle at Guadalcanal, their ship was torpedoed by a Japanese submarine. All of the brothers but George were killed instantly, and he died a short time later while drifting mortally wounded in shark-infested waters, searching in vain for his brothers among other wounded survivors of the blast. The stunned country mourned for the fallen brothers and their bereaved parents, who had suffered the greatest wartime loss of any American family. Because of the great sacrifice of the Sullivan family, a destroyer was named in their honor three months after the tragedy. The USS *The Sullivans* saw intense combat from 1943 through 1965, when it was decommissioned. Yet despite many heated battles, not a soul was lost. Perhaps the shamrocks that were painted on the smokestack because the Sullivan tragedy had occurred on Friday the thirteenth brought the crew luck. Or perhaps the Sullivan brothers were watching over "their ship" and protecting its crew. They do seem to be lingering about.

Many people—too many to ignore—have sensed or seen the brothers aboard the USS *The Sullivans*, evidence that they are still sticking together and still believe they will never die. People have seen hazy apparitions, sometimes numbering five together, drifting down the corridors. They've heard the sounds of men playing cards, chains being dragged, and whispers when nobody else is around. Photographs taken of the brothers' portraits come out with unusual white spots blocking out George's image, as if setting him apart from the others since he wasn't with them at the time of passing. And a security guard once saw the wounded George's ghastly apparition floating on deck. The man promptly quit because of the scare it gave him. Hatches come unlocked, objects shake and rock for no apparent reason, and visitors have reported that they've felt as if they were being choked while in the crew quarters.

In 1965, the ship was donated to New York State as a memorial and museum. You can visit it—and its ghosts—at the Buffalo and Erie County Naval and Servicemen's Park.

Southern
New York

SOUTHERN NEW YORK INCLUDES THE LEGEND-LADEN HUDSON VALLEY and Catskill regions. Washington Irving immortalized these regions with his enchanting tales based on actual people and places he knew here, especially in Sleepy Hollow. Today some say that Irving—the man who wrote America's favorite ghost story—has become a ghost himself, haunting his Sunnyside residence-turned-museum in Tarrytown. Besides the recognition brought to this mountainous, mystical region by Irving's "Rip Van Winkle" and "Legend of Sleepy Hollow," it was also renowned during the Revolutionary War for its many strategic and highly desirable locations, such as West Point and Bannerman's Island—both haunted by ghosts of soldiers past.

The strong supernatural aura of the entire region is further strengthened by reports of encounters with other mysterious beings: Bigfoot-like creatures at Kinderhook, gnomes of the Catskills, and extraterrestrials at the famous Pine Bush UFO hot spot, to name a few. When you enter the Southern New York region, you enter a legendary world of enchantment where anything can happen.

Bannerman's Island

The tiny island officially called Pollepel, but commonly known as Bannerman's, for its most illustrious owner, has been dubbed a "jewel of the Hudson Highlands." Like many jewels, the island does seem to be rich (in its history), enticing, and capable of mysterious powers. Early Native American tribes were so certain the island was haunted by powerful spirits bent on keeping the living away that for many years they refused to set foot on its banks. They saw how the island denied access to all who sought it, protecting itself with strange undercurrents, choppy waters, and reckless winds to drive inquisitive souls away—or swallow them whole. For the same reason, early Dutch explorers claimed that the island was inhabited by goblins and fiends. But that didn't stop Scotsman Francis Bannerman from purchasing the island in 1900 for storage of his massive collection of surplus war stock, which included 90 percent of the surplus of captured equipment and ammunition from the Spanish-American War.

Bannerman's international armory was world renowned. Because of the volume of his acquisitions and the fact that many of his goods, such as black powder, were very volatile, he was forced to move Bannerman's Arsenal first from Brooklyn to 501 Broadway, and finally to the secure, six-and-a-half-acre, midriver haven on the Hudson.

The island, a thousand feet offshore between Breakneck Ridge and Storm King Mountain, first came into prominence during the American Revolution, when pointed, iron-tipped logs were stood on end in the surrounding waters in a failed attempt to hinder the British advance into the Hudson Highlands. General George Washington later approved the construction of a military prison and weapon-storage site on the remote, inhospitable island, but little documentation exists to prove the completion or usage of those facilities. For a time, locals actually enjoyed the island as a recreational site for picnicking, camping, and even swimming. Then Thomas Taft bought it to use as headquarters for his black-market liquor-trading operation.

When the Bannerman dynasty purchased the island from Taft, they had big things in mind. Bannerman and two of his sons set about constructing Bannerman Castle, in which to store their vast collection of marketable and historic weapons and ammunition. Along with the authentically styled Scottish castle, designed by Bannerman himself in homage to his homeland and heritage, they built a family house on top of the hill overlooking the island. It, too, looked much like a Scottish castle. Lucky Bannerman family members spent many summers enjoying the view from the highest point on the island—the same view used by later Indian tribes to spot unsuspecting river travelers before an ambush and by American patriots to spot approaching British invaders during the Revolution. A second house, a lodge, three additional storage buildings, workshops, workmen's apartments, a powder house, and an icehouse rounded out the elaborate Bannerman Arsenal warehouse community.

Bannerman's plan for constructing docks was ingenious. He bought old ships, sank them next to his island, and then covered them with concrete. One such transaction apparently came back to haunt him. A tugboat captain specifically requested that Bannerman's workers wait until he was out of view before sinking his beloved vessel. No captain wants to see his ship go down. Unfortunately, they did not heed his request. He had not even turned away before his tugboat started going down. The captain cursed Bannerman and his crew and warned them that they hadn't heard the last of him. Sure enough, years later, when a lodge was built over the sunken vessel, workers heard a ship's bell double ringing, which means that it was going in reverse. Was the angry captain trying to get his tugboat out of its watery grave and away from the island? The workers certainly entertained that idea.

In 1967, the Bannerman family vacated the island and sold it to the state of New York. Two years later, a mysterious fire ravaged the buildings, leaving the entire island unfit for public visitation. The Bannerman Castle Trust is currently in the process of restoring and preserving the castle and stabilizing other buildings on the island, which is off-limits to the general public because of unsafe conditions.

Christ Episcopal Church

Many people wonder how to reconcile their faith with their belief in the supernatural. They are often surprised to learn that there are actually many haunted churches, and that many men of the cloth have had encounters with ghosts. At Christ Episcopal Church in Poughkeepsie, members of the congregation and the staff have experienced mysterious incidents for quite some time now. The church was founded in 1766, and the structure that now houses its

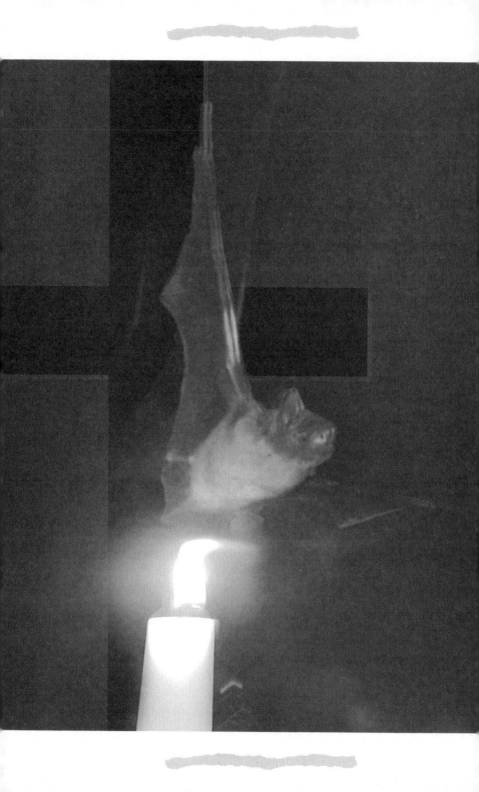

congregation was built on the corner of Academy and Barclay Streets in 1888.

The late Bishop James Pike, who served as rector there in the late 1940s, was the first to admit to seeing a ghost in the church. He believed the ghost was that of a former rector walking up the stairs to the bell and hanging about the altar. During one mass, as he lit a holy candle, Pike was attacked by a bat on the altar. An inexplicable gust of wind blew out the candle just as the bat appeared, according to Susan Smitten's *Ghost Stories of New York State*. The incident was witnessed by the entire congregation. Candles and bats have featured prominently in other strange incidents at Christ Church over the years. The candles in the church library extinguish themselves on occasion, and the malevolent bat has been seen by more than one churchgoer. The fact that it sometimes fades before their eyes gives credence to the possibility that there's something supernatural about the bitter critter.

Such incidents with bats and candles can perhaps be rationalized as not having anything to do with the paranormal; same with doors opening and closing unassisted and occasional odd sounds. But how does one explain away a laughing apparition staring a parishioner in the face? That's just what one woman experienced, as described in Smitten's book. She fell asleep in a church pew while waiting for her sister to finish practicing on the organ one night, when they were the only two in the church, and she woke to see a jovial ghost face looking straight down at her. A number of other people have seen ghosts and shadows on the altar and in other areas of the church.

The hauntings at Christ Episcopal Church have diminished greatly in recent times, and perhaps have stopped altogether. Churchgoers hope that the deceased rectors believed to have haunted the church have finally gone Home.

Eternal Vengeance

One of the stories included in folklorist Charles M. Skinner's 1896 *Myths and Legends of Our Own Land: The Hudson and Its Hills*, "A Trapper's Ghastly Vengeance," was set in Coxsackie in the Catskills in the 1700s. Most of his stories are a mixture of fact and fiction, though some are entirely true and others are pure legend. This one, if true, just goes to show that the truth can be stranger than fiction—and more morbid than anything Stephen King or Wes Craven could conjure.

Hunter and trapper Nick Wolsey lived alone with his dog in a cabin about a mile from the Hudson River, at Coxsackie. While visiting an Indian camp in the wilderness, he became enamored with one of the girls, named Minamee. After many visits, he eventually won her hand in marriage. They had a simple tribal marriage ceremony, but the wedding was disrupted when an Indian who had loved Minamee, yet never let her know his feelings, was overcome with jealousy and attacked Wolsey with a knife. He would have killed the trapper had not Wolsey's faithful dog leaped at the brave and knocked him down. "Wolsey disarmed the fellow and kicked and cuffed him to the edge of the wood," says Skinner, "while the whole company shouted with laughter at this ignominious punishment and approved it."

Wolsey took his wife home to his cabin, and a year or more passed, during which the happy couple had a baby. As Skinner tells it, "Wolsey was seldom absent from his cabin for any considerable length of time and usually returned to it before the night set in." But their simple, happy life was not to last. "One evening he noticed that the grass and twigs were bent near his house by some passing foot that, with the keen eye of the woodman, he saw was not his wife's." He brushed it off, thinking that some hunter had stopped to look at the strange cabin while passing by. A few days later, he returned to find a fresh set of footprints leading to the cabin, and the dead body of his dog lying rigid near the door. Skinner's eerie narrative continues:

"How did this happen, Minamee?" he cried, as he flung open the door. The wife answered in a low voice, "Oh, hush! You'll wake the child."

Nick Wolsey entered the cabin and stood as one turned to marble. Minamee, his wife, sat on the gold hearth, her face and hands cut and blackened, her dress torn, her eyes glassy, a meaningless smile on her lips. In her arms she pressed the body of her infant, its dress soaked with blood, and the head of the little creature lay on the floor beside her. She crooned softly over the cold clay as if hushing it to sleep, and when Wolsey at length found words, she only whispered, "Hush! You will wake him." The night went heavily on; day dawned, and the crooning became lower and lower. Still, through all that day, the bereft woman rocked to and fro upon the floor, and the agonized husband hung about her, trying in vain to give comfort, to bind her wounds, to get some explanation of the mystery that confronted him. The second night set in, and it was evident that it would be the last for Minamee. Her strength failed until she allowed herself to be placed on a couch of skins, while the body of her child was gently lifted from her arms. Then, for a few brief minutes, her reason was restored, and she found words to tell her husband how the Indian whose murderous attack he had thwarted at the wedding had come to the cabin, shot the dog that had rushed out to defend the place, beat the woman back from the door, tore the baby from its bed, slashed its head off with a knife, and, flinging the little body into her lap, departed with the words, "This is my revenge. I am satisfied." Before the sun was in the east again, Minamee was with her baby.

Wolsey sat there for hours. Then he finally arose, saddled his horse, and rode off to Minamee's village. He told the assembled tribe about the heinous deeds, demanding that they hand the murderer over to him. The murderous Indian had expected his people to protect him, but they turned him over to Wolsey, who bound his arms to his side with a rawhide rope and put a noose around his neck. Wolsey tied the other end of it to his saddle and set off for the Hudson, with the Indian forced to walk and run behind the horse. Thus he rode all night, towing the murderer along behind, until they reached the trapper's cabin the next day. Here it was, that Wolsey wreaked his vengeance for the brutal murders of his wife and baby:

Tying his prisoner to a tree, the trapper cut a quantity of young willows, from which he fashioned a large, cradle-like receptacle; in this he placed the culprit, face upward, and tied so stoutly that he could not move a finger; then going into his house, he emerged with the body of Minamee and laid it, face downward, on the wretch, who could not repress a groan of horror as the awful burden sank on his breast. Wolsey bound together the living and the dead, and with a swing of his powerful arms, he flung them on his horse's back, securing them there with so many turns of rope that nothing could displace them. Now he began to lash his horse until the poor beast trembled with anger and pain, when, flinging off the halter, he gave it a final lash, and the animal plunged, foaming and snorting, into the wilderness. When it had vanished and the hoof-beats were no longer heard, Nick Wolsey took his rifle on his arm and left his home forever.

And tradition says that the horse never stopped in its mad careen, but that on still nights, it can be heard sweeping through the woods along the Hudson and along the Mohawk like a whirlwind, and that as the sound goes by, a smothered voice breaks out in cursing, in appeal, then in harsh and dreadful laughter.

Giant Ghost Pig

Many people breathe a sigh of relief when they find out that a particularly unsettling story is, in fact, just a legend. But the funny thing about legends is that sometimes they turn out to be real many years later, when the means of verifying them become available. I once wrote about a well-known legend regarding the Plumbrook Milling Company in Russell, New York. The story goes that a disgruntled miller killed the maiden he loved when he learned that she was in love with someone else, and he allegedly ground her bones, along with those of her lover. Nobody knows for certain what really happened that day, more than a century ago, because the miller, the maiden, and her lover all disappeared without a trace, leading to pure speculation and the stuff legends are made of.

After I wrote that piece, a team of paranormal investigators visited the isolated location where the mill once stood to take soil samples, spirit recordings (audio recordings to detect voice phenomena), and photographs. The results of their investigation were amazing. One photograph clearly showed three orbs, balls of energy thought to be the most basic form in which a spirit manifests: one for the miller, one for the maiden, and one for the maiden's lover. The results of the audio recording were even more exciting. Out in the middle of a wide-open field, far from any traffic noise or other interference, the sound of a woman softly singing was captured on cassette. The investigators were all male. There seemed to be no explanation other than the ghost of the fair maiden who had met her end there. So keep an open mind when reading the following legend about a giant ghost pig, silly as it may sound. Nobody has seen him in a while, but that doesn't mean he never existed, or that he isn't still out there somewhere in the Fishkill region, waiting for the chance to be heard and confirmed on a spirit recording.

Willa Skinner, the Fishkill town historian, has often told the chilling tale of a giant ghost pig said to haunt the Dry Brook area of Albany Post Road near Fishkill. It's been more than a hundred years since the pig was reported to chase stagecoaches and terrorize passing horses, but at one time it happened so frequently that people started calling the area Spook Hollow or Hell Hollow. One poor witness to the frightening apparition said, in words oft repeated, that the swine actually split in two when it approached, with its head moving ahead of the wagon and its back end trailing behind, and then it came back together with a loud clap before vanishing. The pig wasn't the only bizarre ghost seen on Albany Post Road back then. Many people reported a drunken headless horseman who jumped on the backs of wagons and stagecoaches and rummaged for whiskey. As he went about his spectral business, he repeated, "Jug-o'-rum, jug-o'-rum." Now *that* would make a great recording to provide evidence of the legendary specters of the Dry Brook area.

Kinderhook Creature

By the time *Monsters of the North Woods,* by Robert Bartholomew et al., was released in the early 1990s, there had been at least 114 documented sightings of Bigfoot-like creatures in New York State alone. Reports dated back to the ancient Native American days, when such creatures were called Windigo by New York's Algonquin tribe, Stone Giants by the Iroquois, and Gougou by the Micmac.

Nearly every region of New York State has reported sightings of Bigfoot: a "wild man" that came out of the woods of Sackets Harbor in 1818; sightings in 1893 of an aggressive "wild man" in Rockaway, Long Island; a Bigfoot-like creature crossing the road in Rouses Point in the 1950s; a similar creature seen during a UFO flap in Ithaca in 1967; and a wave of Whitehall sightings accompanied by enormous footprints left by the creature in 1976.

The small, haunted town of Kinderhook is the Hudson Valley region's Bigfoot hangout, or at least it was. Between 1978 and 1988, it had twenty-one sightings that fell into the Bigfoot category, according to *Monsters of the North Woods.* The Kinderhook creatures—occasionally seen in groups of three or more—were described by the same adjectives over and over: big, black, hairy, seven to eight feet tall, red-eyed, matted, and hulking. Most often, the Kinderhook Bigfoot appeared to have black fur or hair; however, several people witnessed creatures that were reddish brown in color, and a few saw ones that were solid white. The Kinderhook sightings were often accompanied by eerie sounds that some have compared to a woman shrieking, a baby crying, a shrill scream, a pig squealing, monkey babble, or grunting. The strange vocalizations seemed to be in response to the creatures feeling cornered or possibly sounding an alarm to others of their tribe, assuming they had one. They also often screamed while retreating back into the woods or wherever they hid.

Some people saw something that may have been an altogether different being—even though it was reported at the height of Bigfoot sightings. That entity was described as a "white blob" that seemed to peek out from behind a tree on one occasion and glide down a hill toward its terrified witnesses on another. A phantom Bigfoot? That would explain the lack of footprints in places where Bigfoot was known to have trod . . . not to mention the lack of ever finding a Bigfoot skeleton. Many believe there may be a link between Bigfoot sightings and UFOs or ghosts, or both. Paranormal phenomena of every kind increase in the immediate vicinity of active Bigfoot sightings—not just at Kinderhook, but around the world—so there may be something to that opinion.

Lack of footprints wasn't a problem in Kinderhook, though. With many sightings in such a concentrated area, large tracks and footprints were easily located all around the Kinderhook area. The Bigfoot investigations in that Hudson Valley town provided researchers worldwide with many excellent photographs and casts of giant footprints to study and interpret.

Night Riders

The town of Copake is in Taconic State Park, among the Berkshire Hills, and it is there that a wizard, said to have been partnered with the Devil himself, once lived a couple hundred years ago. Francis Woolcott was tall, dark, and sinister, and his teeth protruded when he gave his horrible laugh. According to folklorist Charles M. Skinner's 1896 *Myths and Legends of Our Own Land: The Hudson and Its Hills,* that laugh "used to give his neighbors a creep along their spines." Though the man had no obvious occupation, he had no trouble acquiring the necessities—pork, flour, meal, and cider— because the farmers feared him so much that they would give him anything to keep him from casting a dreadful spell on them or their animals. As Skinner describes it:

> He could have what he chose for the asking, for had he not halted horses at the plow so that neither blows nor commands could move them for two hours? Had he not set farmer Raught's pigs to walking on their hind legs and trying to talk? When he shouted, "Hup! Hup! Hup!" to farmer Williams' children, had they not leaped to the molding of the parlor wainscot—a yard above the floor and only an inch wide—and walked around it, afterward skipping like birds from chair-back to chair-back while the furniture stood as if nailed to the floor? And was he not the chief of thirteen night-riders, whose faces no man had seen, nor wanted to see, and whom he sent about the country on errands of mischief every night when the moon was growing old? As to moans, had he not found a mystic message from our satellite on Mount Riga, graven on a meteor?

He must have been a devil, or a monster, or a witch—for who else would have thirteen (a symbolic of bad luck) faceless night riders do his deeds? Skinner relates that the evil deeds included horses tails being tied, hogs foaming at the mouth and walking like men, and cows giving blood instead of milk. The night riders met Woolcott in a grove of trees, carrying stolen bundles of oat straw, which Woolcott changed to black horses after dark.

> These horses could not cross streams of water, and on the stroke of midnight, they fell to pieces and were oaten sheaves once more, but during their time of action, they rushed through woods, bearing the riders safely, and tore like hurricanes across the fields, leaping bushes, fences, even trees, without effort. Never could traces be found of them the next day.

Skinner also reports a series of strange events that accompanied Woolcott's death:

> At last the Devil came to claim his own. Woolcott, who was ninety years old, lay sick and helpless in his cabin. Clergymen refused to see him, but two or three of his neighbors stifled their fears and went to the wizard's house to soothe his dying moments. With the

night came storm, and with its outbreak, the old man's face took on such a strange and horrible look that the watchers fell back in alarm. There was a burst of purple flame at the window, a frightful peak, a smell of sulphur, and Woolcott was dead. When the watchers went out, the roads were dry, and none of the village had heard wind, rain, or thunder. It was the coming of the fiend. . .

The Ackley House

"As a matter of law, the house is haunted." With those now legendary words, the gavel sounded, and real-estate agents would never look at haunted property the same way again. In 1991, the Appellate Division of the New York State Supreme Court ruled that real-estate agents were required by law to inform potential buyers that a home was haunted, if that information was made known to them by the seller. It was not the buyer's responsibility to determine if a home was haunted in the relatively short amount of time they viewed it prior to purchase. It was the property owner's responsibility to inform the agent or buyer, and it was the agent's responsibility to inform the potential buyer, if the property owner hadn't.

By the mid-1990s, however, New York State passed the Stigmatized Property Laws, which considerably eased the burden on real-estate agents by requiring them to divulge only information regarding physical defects of the home, not intangible points, such as on-site murders and suicides . . . or alleged paranormal activity. The jury is still out on whether it's better to tell all or to withhold such potentially damaging information from prospective buyers and hope that they never find out.

When Jeffrey and Patrice Stambovsky bought Helen Ackley's well-known haunted manor in Nyack, they were informed by locals shortly after they signed the papers and made a sizable down payment on the property that they had bought a haunted house. They learned that their new home had been featured in a story in the May 1977 *Reader's Digest* and was even included in the local ghost tour of haunted homes. It boasted several ghosts, according to Ackley. One watched her paint her living room and nodded his approval; another shook her daughter awake each morning for school; mysterious small gifts appeared on special occasions, though nobody knew where they came from; one jolly ghost reminded Ackley of Santa Claus; and others she saw were dressed in Revolutionary War–era clothing.

Realizing their dream home could quickly become a nightmare—both psychologically and for future resale—they attempted to renege on the real-estate transaction and get their down payment back, but Ackley refused to refund it. The Stambovskys took the matter all the way to the top—the New York State Supreme Court—and eventually the court agreed that the transaction should be null and void, and the Stambovskys should be refunded most of their down payment. The reason? Ackley had actively promoted her house as being a haunted property, basking in the glow of the attention it brought, but she failed to inform the buyers that her property was famously haunted and thus stigmatized for future owners. Because of her efforts to make her house a *known* haunted house, the court decided that "as a matter of law, the house [was] haunted."

The Hudson Valley UFO Flap

Just before midnight on New Year's Eve 1982, while thousands were looking toward the sky in Times Square in anticipation of the famous ball dropping, there was an entirely different—though just as spectacular—aerial display in the sky over nearby Kent, a small town one hour north of New York City. Not only did the stroke of midnight herald in the New Year, but it also marked the commencement of a UFO flap in the Hudson Valley that would last for five years.

A retired police officer was the first to report a strange grouping of multicolored lights moving slowly and silently over the Hudson Valley area. He watched as the V-shaped row of lights approached and passed over his house so slowly that he could see the triangular spacecraft it was attached to. The only sound the object made was a low hum. Similar reports continued to pour in from hundreds of witnesses over the next few years, and a UFO hotline was opened up that received more than three hundred calls from people who saw a UFO on March 24, 1983, alone. That sighting was reported on the front page of the *Westchester-Rockland Daily Item*, with the headline "Hundreds Claim to Have Seen UFO." Public interest became so great that Dr. J. Allen Hynek, founder of the Center for UFO Studies, along with Philip Imbrogno and Bob Pratt, wrote a book documenting the flap called *Night Siege: The Hudson Valley UFO Sightings.*

One witness described the flying saucer he observed as a "flying city" because of its immense size. Another who saw it zigzagging over the Taconic Parkway said it was as big as an aircraft carrier. Yet another person described it as the size of three football fields. The object or objects typically glided along slowly and almost silently, sometimes hovering and other times zooming away at speeds not yet possible with earthly technology. At one point, an enormous boomerang-shaped craft hovered over the Newburgh mall in broad daylight in an incident so compelling that it was featured on an episode of *Unsolved Mysteries.*

Blimps were considered to be a possible explanation for the multitude of sightings, because of their ability to move slowly and hover, but that idea was quickly ruled out. Most people were able to see the triangular shape of the fuselage, and no blimps occupied airspace at the time of the sightings over the Hudson Valley. Eventually law enforcement's official statement was that the objects causing all the excitement were simply ultralight aircraft flying in formation out of the nearby Stormville Airport, but the many people who saw the objects up close knew better. For them the entire incident remains a mystery, and it helped secure the Hudson Valley's place at the top of the list of UFO hot spots, not only in New York State, but worldwide.

A small town with barely eight thousand citizens, Pine Bush has made a big name for itself in the annals of ufology. Known as the "UFO Capital of the Northeast," it was put on the map about twenty years ago when ufologists decided that Pine Bush had to be some sort of an interdimensional gateway because it was so laden with extraterrestrial activity. Reported phenomena included sightings of strange lights in the sky that appeared to be attached to triangular or boomerang-shaped spacecraft; photographs of Tesla globes, which look much like spectral orbs; and alien encounters and abductions. At the same time, there was an increase in other paranormal matters, such as sightings of Bigfoot-like creatures, phenomena at haunted locales, and poltergeist activity.

Hudson Valley resident Whitley Streiber wrote several books about his abduction by aliens from his cabin near Pine Bush, including the smash hit *Communion.* Reports of sightings, encounters, and abductions related to UFOs in the Pine Bush area peaked in 1993. Several regional books with widespread appeal have since been released on the topic. The area is quieter these days, with reports of sightings more sporadic, allowing the media hype to die down considerably. But the town will forever be thought of as UFO Central to those in the know, and its residents are already prepared for the next wave of sightings. If you're interested in the ultimate Pine Bush experience, you can visit the UFO-themed Burlingham Inn UFO Bed and Breakfast and the Cup and Saucer diner.

The Real Sleepy Hollow

One of the greatest ghost stories ever told was Washington Irving's "Legend of Sleepy Hollow," a short story that was part of a collection of tales published in a tome called *The Sketch Book of Geoffrey Crayon, Gent,* in 1820. The fictional story is so well known that its characters are practically household names: Ichabod Crane, the timid and hapless schoolmaster; Brom Bones, the local tough guy who set Crane up; Katrina Van Tassel, the young woman both men loved; and the Headless Horseman. Bones was intent on getting Crane out of town, and out of the way, so that he could have Katrina's attention all to himself. So he fabricated a story about the ghost of a headless Hessian soldier that appeared on the very route Crane would take home, hoping that Crane's imagination would get the better of him as he passed the dreaded area where dwelt the headless horseman, and that he would then flee from town, never to return. That was the plan, and it worked.

The climax to the story took place as Ichabod Crane came upon the alleged area of the haunting and realized he was not alone; something supernatural seemed amiss:

> There was something in the moody and dogged silence of this pertinacious companion that was mysterious and appalling. It was soon fearfully accounted for. On mounting a rising ground, which brought the figure of his fellow-traveler in relief against the sky, gigantic in height, and muffled in a cloak, Ichabod was horrorstruck on perceiving that he was headless!—but his horror was still more increased, on observing that the head, which should have rested on his shoulders, was carried before him on the pommel of the saddle; his terror rose to desperation; he rained a

shower of kicks and blows upon Gunpowder; hoping, by a sudden movement, to give his companion the slip—but the spectre started full jump with him. Away they dashed, through the thick and thin; stones flying, and sparks flashing at every bound. Ichabod's flimsy garments fluttered in the air, as he stretched his long lanky body away over his horse's head, in the eagerness of his flight.

And away over the Sleepy Hollow Bridge—also called the Headless Horseman Bridge—they raced, disappearing into the night, as the legend goes.

Sleepy Hollow, known as North Tarrytown until 1996, is a small town of about eight thousand residents on the left bank of the Hudson River just twenty-five miles north of Manhattan. Irving, a former resident of the town, based the settings and characters of both "The Legend of Sleepy Hollow" and "Rip Van Winkle" on his impressions of the place and the people of that time. His Rip Van Winkle took a twenty-year nap at Sleepy Hollow and awoke to find many changes. But the real Sleepy Hollow, though settled in 1640, has not changed as much as one might expect of a village in such close proximity to one of the world's largest urban centers, New York City. It's a town that's strangely—perhaps magically—untouched by time. For that reason, Irving's description of Sleepy Hollow in his legend of the same name is, in many ways, as true today as it was in his day:

A drowsy, dreamy influence seems to hang over the land, and to pervade the very atmosphere. Some say that the place was bewitched by a high German doctor during the early days of the settlement; others, that an old Indian chief, the prophet or wizard of his tribe, held his powwows there before the country was discovered by Master Henrick Hudson. Certain it is, the place still continues under the sway of some witching power that holds a spell over the minds of the good people, causing them to walk in a continual reverie. They are given to all kinds of marvelous beliefs; are subject to trances and visions; and frequently see strange sights and hear music and voices in the air. The whole neighborhood abounds with local tales, haunted spots, and twilight superstitions.

Indeed, Washington Irving himself is now said to haunt his famous abode, called Sunnyside, a Dutch farmhouse he bought in 1835 in the nearby village of Irvington. Today it is a tourist attraction where interpreters dressed in period clothing greet visitors who can delight in seeing the author's original books, as well as personal belongings and memorabilia. If they're really lucky, they might catch a glimpse of Irving's ghost, who is said to haunt the place, occasionally pinching female visitors in a mischievous way. His nephew told of seeing Irving's ghost walk through the living room, where the man sat with his daughters, and straight into his old study. Irving's nieces, who once lived with him, are also said to haunt Sunnyside, cleaning up after the last worker leaves for the day.

The Riotous Catskill Gnomes

The twenty-year-long sleep of Washington Irving's Rip Van Winkle character was preceded by an encounter with some strange characters called the Catskill Gnomes. Irving's story may have been based loosely on fact. The following brief account of some Catskill people said to be dwarfed because of a type of liquor they drank is from folklorist Charles M. Skinner's 1896 *Myths and Legends of Our Own Land: The Hudson and Its Hills:*

> Behind the New Grand Hotel in the Catskills is an amphitheatre of mountain that is held to be the place of which the Mohicans spoke when they told of people there who worked in metals and had bushy beards and eyes like pigs. From the smoke of their forges in autumn came the haze of Indian summer; and when the moon was full, it was their custom to assemble on the edge of a precipice above the hollow and dance and caper until the night was nigh worn away. They brewed a liquor that had the effect of shortening the bodies and swelling the heads of all who drank it, and when Hudson and his crew visited the mountains, the pygmies held a carouse in his honor and invited him to drink their liquor. The crew went away, shrunken and distorted by the magic distillation, and thus it was that Rip Van Winkle found them on the eve of his famous sleep.

And we all know what happened when he drank the magic distillation . . . but at least he didn't shrink.

West Point Military Academy

Constructed in 1778, the West Point Military Academy is the nation's oldest continuously operating military post. It served as Washington's headquarters during the American Revolution and has since housed such historic military figures as General (later President) Ulysses S. Grant and General Robert E. Lee. Some of its more prominent graduates include Dwight D. Eisenhower, Douglas MacArthur, George S. Patton—and Edgar Allan Poe, the master of horror himself. Poe reveled in the ghost stories associated with his alma mater, even if he had nothing to do with the stories himself.

Over the years, ghosts have been reported from time to time at the academy. One man was awakened by a beautiful woman in a long, white dress standing over his bed—not a bad thing to be woken up to, if the woman was alive, but this one definitely was a ghost, as she walked straight through the door. Some believe it may have been an Irish cook named Molly who worked for the "Father of the Military Academy," Colonel Sylvanus Thayer. Others say perhaps it was the wife of a professor who actually married her mother after his wife died. She was thought to have chased several young girls from the Morrison House on the grounds in the 1920s.

Other inexplicable things have happened as well, such as beds that were found rumpled up—and everyone knows how precisely beds are made in the military. Objects and valuables have been misplaced and later discovered where they shouldn't be. Showers have turned on by themselves. But the most famous paranormal incident at the academy took place in 1972. Several honorable cadets of Company G-4 were in Room 4714 in the 47th Division Barracks of the 4th Regiment when an apparition manifested before their eyes. It appeared to be a soldier dressed in a cavalry uniform from the 1830s and holding a musket rifle. The shimmering ghost, who sported a handlebar mustache, came out of the wall near the closet, turned, and walked back through the wall. The entire incident was preceded by a sudden drop in room temperature felt by all present. Another time, in the same room, a ghost was seen starting to rise up out of the floor. By mid-November of that year, the commanding officer, knowing his cadets were prohibited from lying under the Cadet Honor Code, had the room turned into a storage-only room. And it remains unoccupied to this day . . . at least by the living.

New York City

They don't call it "the city that never sleeps" for nothing. With eight million residents crammed into such close quarters, it's a wonder anyone is able to rest in peace in Manhattan and its surrounds. The energy here is unparalleled, and time, which seems to stand still in the nearby Hudson Valley and Catskills, rushes by in a "New York minute." In the world of the paranormal, there are at least two other things that seem to manipulate time and energy like that: ghosts and UFOs. And our nation's largest city has its fair share of both, including the Brooklyn Bridge alien abduction; the Great Northeast Power Blackout, which coincided with UFO sightings over the city; and the many haunted Broadway theaters, former speakeasies, inns, townhouses, hotels, and bistros. You name it— New York City is up to its skyscrapers in strange sights and supernatural phenomena.

Chumley's

Leland "Lee" Chumley knew how to get a job done. His well-rounded employment history undoubtedly contributed to the enduring success of his final venture—a speakeasy for the literary elite of New York City. As an artist, cartoonist, and editorial writer, Chumley knew the importance of having a place where like minds could socialize and indulge in a little inebriation once in a while to help get their creative juices flowing. He also had a reputation in organized labor and was well versed in drawing people together toward a common goal. He was definitely up to the job of being an owner and operator of a successful speakeasy. But his was not just any old speakeasy—though it *was* old, and it's now the oldest and only surviving speakeasy left in New York City.

The building was originally a Federal-style home built in 1831 at 86 Bedford Street, its official address, but don't look for an entrance at that door. It wasn't until 1922 that Chumley found his niche and converted the home and onetime blacksmith shop into an instantly prosperous speakeasy with a secret, isolated entrance on Barrow Street, which remains the unmarked main entrance to the building today. There is no outdoor sign for the real entrance to Chumley's, nor has there ever been. But that didn't stop an impressive list of famous literary and creative geniuses from finding their way to its hidden door during Prohibition.

The atmosphere inside Chumley's is very friendly and relaxed. Hundreds of book covers and photographs of notable guests such as F. Scott Fitzgerald, Edna St. Vincent Millay, Orson Welles, and Upton Sinclair grace the tavern's walls today, reminding modern patrons of those who frequented the bar in its early, covert days. According to many, there are other, less tangible reminders of visitors who have passed through—and passed on—including Chumley's alleged wife, Henrietta, who nobody even knew existed until shortly after her husband died, when she showed up at the bar one day and announced that she was the new owner.

Following the passing of her husband, Henrietta was at the speakeasy every night, overseeing business from her table in front of the fireplace, drinking until she passed out, then being carried home by the hired help. Some believe she continues to watch over business, showing annoyance at renovations and updates by manipulating objects such as the jukebox and pinball machine. During a tour of New York City pubs, one tour group was treated to a phantom tantrum when bottles and glasses started falling off the bar shelves, even though nobody was near them. The bartender calmly went about his business, telling the group that it was just Mrs. Chumley.

Owner Steve Shlopak has seen his share of mysterious events at Chumley's, but he believes the paranormal incidents involve spirits from the not-too-distant past, such as deceased firefighters who continue to help their friend with matters of the physical world from their spirit dimension. Shlopak's close friend and firefighter Captain John Drennan, whose picture hangs over the bar, died in a fire rescue attempt in 1994. At the same time, Shlopak had just lost his business partner and was pondering what direction he would take at Chumley's. Shortly thereafter, seven firefighters from Engine 24, Ladder 5, showed up at his place to help out their friend. He kept them on as staff and has had an all-firefighter crew ever since. Now he believes some of those firefighters who have since passed on, including sixteen who died in the World Trade Center attack in 2001, continue to visit the pub in spirit form. There have been too many strange incidents to chalk it up to sheer coincidence.

When Shlopak and the other firefighter staff are conversing about any given subject, they sometimes hear the jukebox playing a song with lyrics pertinent to that particular discussion. Once when some of the men were talking about the memorial services of one of their comrades, the words, "We're on the road again, we're on the way to paradise," drifted through the room from the jukebox—which wasn't even plugged in at the time. The staff never plugged it in until just before opening at four in the afternoon. That incident was enough to make three of the stunned employees quickly eighty-six it. This phrase may actually have originated at Chumley's during its Prohibition days. When the police were trying to raid the building through the fake entrance at 86 Bedford, someone would alert the law-breaking patrons to "eighty-six it," meaning to run for the exits. Since that time, the phrase has taken on additional meanings in restaurants and bars, causing confusion as to where it actually originated.

The innocence of incidents like the jukebox episode, baffling as they are, have convinced Shlopak that his beloved historic bar is haunted merely by spirits of the dearly departed, not some disgruntled ghost with a bone to pick.

Manhattan Bistro

In 1799, three days before Christmas, a beautiful young hatmaker named Elma was murdered. Her boyfriend, a shameless player, allegedly committed the deed and then stuffed her body in a well at the intersection of Spring and Greene Streets. The young man was accused, but his very rich uncle hired the best attorneys—Alexander Hamilton and Aaron Burr. The jury believed the young man's pathetic stories and his lawyers' claims that the woman was suicidal and had brought the tragedy on herself, so he was quickly released. Fellow citizens were not happy with the verdict, however, and they hounded and threatened the young man until he finally left New York City. But the unfortunate victim remains, in spirit.

For many years, the well in which the woman had been found was thought to have disappeared, probably removed to a dump or having sunk to the bottom of the river. Nobody still alive was aware of its location until the owner of the Manhattan Bistro, Marie DaGrossa, had the basement to her establishment, which had been filled in with dirt many years before, dug up to make way for an addition to the thriving business. That was when she discovered the unusual relic. Knowing her building was built in 1850, she sought the expertise of the Landmarks Conservancy. That's when she learned that her basement was the final resting place of the infamous well in which the murdered woman's body had been placed in 1799, and as such, it was also the final resting place of the young lady herself—which may explain the curious apparitions and supernatural phenomena that occur from time to time in the building.

Both the manager and the owner of the Manhattan Bistro agree that something strange is going on at the bar and restaurant, although the owner is quick to admit that she is not sure whether she believes in ghosts. Still, how does one explain ashtrays flying off the tables so forcefully that they smash into the walls, bottles occasionally flying off the shelves, plates falling off the tables, and lights turning on and off by themselves? Even more difficult to explain are the apparitions of a woman, always with long hair, just like Elma. Sometimes her spirit is seen at the location where her body was originally dumped on Spring Street, and her chilling apparition is aged and covered with seaweed and goop. Other times she appears at bedsides in the area in the middle of the night, wearing a long gown. One artist was so mesmerized by the apparition of a graceful young woman with long hair that she saw outside her window that she painted a series of canvases depicting her sightings, according to Susan Smitten's *Ghost Stories of New York State.*

So often has her apparition been seen that it's known in occult circles as the Spring Street Ghost.

Then there are the sightings in the Bistro's basement, where the round brick well is still located. Workers swore they saw a spiraling mist swirl out from the well one day. Thankfully, that's the only possible sighting of Elma's ghost inside the Manhattan Bistro, but that's not to say that she isn't there. Could the flying objects and other phenomena be the result of an occasional harmless tantrum, as Elma reminds everyone that she's there, she's angry, and she's still unable to rest? How many times has failed justice caused an unhappy, innocent spirit to stay behind?

Old Bermuda Inn

Besides being one of the most romantic restaurants on Staten Island, the Old Bermuda Inn is also one of its most haunted establishments. And Martha Mesereau is one of the borough's most famous ghosts.

Martha and her husband built the two-story mansion at 2512 Arthur Kill Road as a summer residence shortly before Mr. Mesereau was called into service during the Civil War. Upon hearing that her husband was missing in action, the twenty-seven-year-old Martha became so distraught that she became reclusive, hiding in an upstairs bedroom until she finally died of a broken heart. Her spirit stayed behind, awaiting the return of her husband.

Many people have seen a ghost that they presume to be Martha, wandering about the second floor between rooms, and one of the managers said he hears her crying and walking every week. Her apparition has also been seen on the stairs and walking through the five dining areas. After closing, when all the lights have been turned off, one light occasionally turns back on by itself, as if Martha is keeping one candle lit in the window until her husband's safe return. Or perhaps it is her husband's work, calling her lonely spirit into the light . . . where he is waiting for her.

One If by Land, Two If by Sea

One If by Land, Two If by Sea is a Greenwich Village restaurant that has become synonymous with love, a place where a dozen engagements may take place on any given evening. Its elegant atmosphere epitomizes romance, making it a favored place at which to propose. Ah, yes . . . love is in the air here, along with the sensuous aromas wafting from its world-class kitchen. And every once in a while, there's something else in the air that's a little harder to put your finger on—could it be a ghost?

One If by Land, Two If by Sea was built in 1767 on Richmond Hill, now leveled, on the Hudson, but the structure was gutted and relocated to 17 Barrow Street by John Jacob Astor. In its current location, it was used as a theater for a time. After a series of other owners, two enterprising gentlemen, Mario DeMartini and Armand Braiger, purchased it, converted it into a classy romantic restaurant, and opened it as One If by Land, Two If by Sea in 1972. When DeMartini died, Braiger partnered with Noury Gourjjane, and the latter continues to run the business today—with a little help from his friends of the supernatural kind.

People have reported strange and inexplicable things over the years. The manager has heard heavy men's footsteps walking up the stairs to the third floor and then directly overhead of her office, which, incidentally, was a brothel at one time. She also has often heard the sound of clinking glasses coming from the unused third floor, as if someone is making a toast—not an uncommon occurrence at such a restaurant, but impossible coming from an empty room. Another strange sound heard on occasion is a cat meowing, but the restaurant has no cat. One skeptical employee who had tired of hearing the "nonsense" about ghosts was working alone one night, when the copier suddenly started up on its own, going through the sort function. He quit the next day.

The ghosts also have revealed themselves visually, though this hasn't been happening as frequently. But for a while, employees reported seeing a woman in white passing through one level of the building. She was most often seen floating around after hours. She also may be responsible for moving the wall hangings ever so slightly, just enough to let people know she's been there. And perhaps it was her reflection on a tablecloth that puzzled staff and customers one evening. They adjusted the lighting to see if the silhouette of a woman in a long gown would vanish, but it didn't, no matter what they tried.

Because the building at one time belonged to Aaron Burr, serving as his carriage house and stable, some speculate that perhaps it's his daughter, Theodosia, who mysteriously vanished at sea on her way to visit her father there. Others believe she's someone called Elizabeth, who named herself in a recording taken by a team of parapsychologists brought in to investigate. Nobody knew what Elizabeth's ties to the place could have been until the foundation was dug up and two tombstones were unearthed, one bearing the name Elizabeth Seaman.

The restaurant's ghosts are completely harmless and certainly haven't scared customers away. After all, they say it's a place where memories are made. Indeed.

The Belasco Theatre

Originally called the Stuyvesant, Broadway's Belasco Theatre at 111 West Forty-fourth Street opened in 1907 under David Belasco's capable management. Many of its shows over the years, such as *All the Way Home,* Ralph Fiennes's *Hamlet,* and Janet McTeer's *A Doll House,* boasted Tony winners. Other notable shows included *Oh, Calcutta!, Follies,* and *The Rocky Horror Show.* Belasco changed the theater's name to his own in 1910, and even though he died in 1931, the theater, now owned by the Shubert Organization, still goes by the name of Belasco. In the 1940s, the Belasco was the home of the influential Group Theatre; and in the early 1990s, it was home to Tony Randall's National Actors Theatre, according to a Shubert Organization archivist.

David Belasco was a jack-of-all-trades: a producer, playwright, actor, innovative set designer, proprietor, theater manager, impresario, and last but not least, a ghost. He is believed to have haunted his theater virtually since the day he died. His apparition was often seen sitting in his special box from which he watched the shows while alive, and his attire also made his identity obvious. He was nicknamed the Bishop of Broadway for the dark suits and white collars that made up his wardrobe, and the apparition that has been seen over the years is dressed in that same priestly manner. Many people claim that they've seen his ghost sitting in his old seat, frowning during and immediately after opening shows, as if he were disappointed in the performances.

Belasco makes his presence known in other ways. People occasionally smell cigar smoke, presumably his, when nobody is smoking. The private elevator to the theater manager's penthouse suite once operated backstage, accommodating both Belasco and select guests, including an endless supply of eager actress hopefuls he invited to "sit on his casting couch." Although it's been dismantled now for some time, several people, including a stage hand, have heard the rattling of the elevator's old chains, as if it were still in use. Others have heard the sounds of partying emanating from within Belasco's suite when nobody's inside. Less conspicuous clues to the haunted status of the building run the gamut from the stage curtains moving on their own to props disappearing when needed for the shows and reappearing when the performances are over.

Another ghost, this one blue, has appeared high up in the balcony, either as an apparition of a woman wearing a blue gown or as a blue light drifting up what would be the center aisle of the balcony, if it had one. One performer saw the same lady in blue every night during her performance in a part of the show that required her to look up for a few moments. After closing one night, a stagehand witnessed a woman in blue walking across the back of the theater toward the balcony stairs. He and another man were the only people in the building at the time. Another employee saw a blur of blue ascending the steps to Belasco's apartment one night and felt a strong chill go through him at the moment the apparition brushed past. It could not have been solid, because it didn't trip the motion-activated alarm system. The identity of the blue lady may not be as obvious as Belasco's pastoral specter, but it would seem that even in death, Belasco doesn't have to look far to find suitable female companionship.

The Bridge Café

Built in 1794, City Hall/South Street Seaport District's famous Bridge Café, so named in 1979 for its proximity to the Brooklyn Bridge, is said to be the oldest eating and drinking establishment in New York. It also boasts the distinction of being Manhattan's longest-running saloon, serving fine wine—and spirits—continuously at 279 Water Street since 1847. As well, it is the oldest commercial wood-frame building in New York City, even older than Chase Manhattan, which started out as the Manhattan Company in 1799. With credits like that, how could such a historic café not be haunted?

One could speculate on any number of reasons a ghost might be inclined to haunt a building that has seen sea captains, river pirates, prostitutes, murderers, gamblers, and aristocrats pass through its doors over more than two centuries. Was the spectral sea captain who walked through the bar and sat at a stool in front of the mystified manager just passing time until his ghost ship departed? Was the female apparition seen drifting across the room toward the windows overlooking the East River waiting for a ship to come in, unaware that it had come and gone long ago? Did the couple keep passing each other like two ships in the night, eternally searching but never finding? The possibilities one's imagination can conjure are endless.

Adam Weprin's family operates the Bridge Café, and he has heard the unmistakable sound of heavy footsteps overhead on many occasions. Two of those times, there were several witnesses who heard the same thing. The incidents occurred more than a decade apart yet were uncannily similar. Other ghostly phenomena experienced by staff and visitors include equipment malfunctioning, cold drafts drifting past people, keys going missing and being bent when found, and the phone sometimes making a windlike noise while in use. But probably the most intimidating incident occurred when a previous head chef tried to repair a broken refrigerator. As the son of an electrician, he knew to unplug the unit and turn off the breaker switch to avoid any possibility of electrocuting himself. And yet somehow the refrigerator sent a jolt of electricity through him the moment he began his repair work, just enough to stun him—as if the fact that a ghost may have been responsible for it wasn't enough of a shock.

Regardless of its inevitable ghost or two, the Bridge Café is a must-see for city folk and tourists alike. Besides its historic past and ghostly present, the highly favored dining spot at the base of the Brooklyn Bridge serves up superb food in the most authentic atmosphere of yesteryear, no holds barred.

The Brooklyn Bridge Encounter

If ever there was an alien encounter that deserved—indeed, demanded—much more media hype than it was given, it was the remarkable case that became the subject of Budd Hopkins's third book, *Witnessed.*

At approximately 3:15 A.M. on November 30, 1989, Linda Cortile says she was abducted by aliens through the barred window of her twelfth-floor apartment in lower Manhattan. As the story goes, Cortile was taken through the air by several "Greys"—the most common type of aliens encountered by reported abductees. They took her into the belly of a spacecraft that was hovering over her apartment building in plain view of anyone in the vicinity of the Brooklyn Bridge and East River who might notice it despite its camouflage amid the usual light show of the New York City skyline. In fact, in the year that followed, a surprising number of people came forward with information of a UFO sighting that night in the proximity of the Brooklyn Bridge, and some of them even claimed to have seen a woman, escorted by several alien beings, drifting through the air toward the waiting spacecraft.

Besides Cortile, three other people came forward with their own stories of abduction by the same spacecraft that night, including a United Nations entourage that happened to be crossing the Brooklyn Bridge at the time, consisting of a very highly placed UN administrator and his two distinguished bodyguards, whose jobs required level-headedness (a good incentive to keep quiet about the incident). Cortile was taken to the UFO's examination room, physically examined, questioned about her family, and then returned to her bed.

Her full recollections about the incident came out during a hypnosis session with Hopkins, whom she had met earlier that year after reading his book *Intruders,* which described the phenomenon of alien implants. Cortile's doctor had discovered a small surgical scar in her nostril during a routine exam, even though she had never had surgery. Hopkins's book offered a possible, though unimaginable, explanation, so she contacted him and recounted her earliest memories, which seemed to indicate a lifetime of alien encounters.

Her experiences were nothing new to Hopkins, who had studied many people with abduction stories similar to Cortile's. Her case was not at all unusual—that is, until her urgent phone call to his office following the famous Brooklyn Bridge encounter. And the rest, as they say, is history. The Linda Cortile abduction has become New York State's claim to fame in the annals of alien abductions.

The Ear Inn

The Ear Inn at 326 Spring Street is one of the oldest bars in Manhattan, and what a history it has. The building that houses the Ear Inn bar and restaurant is known as the James Brown House, for the original owner, said to be a black man who fought in the American Revolution before settling in at the house and selling tobacco. In 1833, Brown sold his house to two pharmaceutical merchants. Then in the late 1800s, the Brown House was bought by Thomas Cloke, who, along with his brother, made whiskey and beer and sold it to ships on the nearby waterfront. During Prohibition, the house again changed hands and became a speakeasy. It was also during that time that the Holland Tunnel was built, running directly under the Brown House.

In 1969, the Landmarks Preservation Commission designated the house a historic landmark, but that didn't initially change the fact that the entire neighborhood picture was looking dismal because of a decline in shipping at that particular location. The area became run-down and was largely abandoned. In 1973, two students who were renting rooms on the upper floor of the house accepted an offer to buy the place. They fixed it up in a moderate way, as they were of moderate means at the time. To save money, instead of tearing down the sign that read "Bar," they simply painted over the right side of the B, changing it to an E, and ever since it has been known as the Ear Inn. Business picked up for the entrepreneurial pair, with the help of such prominent visitors as John Lennon and Salvador Dali, and business has been great ever since.

Today the Ear Inn is owned by Martin Sheridan and Jerry Walker. The neighborhood continues to improve, and things are really looking up for the pub. Even the fact that it's haunted hasn't slowed business as far as anyone can tell. Mickey, the ghost sailor (and former regular) with a penchant for a pretty face, doesn't scare away the women who board on the upper two floors too often. The fact that he's been known to pinch an occasional female derriére in the bar is a cause more for laughter than for fear. Besides Mickey's apparent pranks, such as shaking the ladies beds in the rooms upstairs that are boarded out, the only other clues that the Ear Inn is haunted are standard fare at paranormally active locations—things like cell phone and camera batteries dying rapidly, electrical equipment malfunctioning occasionally. But there's nothing the owners and customers need worry too much about. The fact of the matter is that the Ear Inn's ghost only adds to its colorful history and charm.

The Gay Street Phantom

It should be no surprise that there's a Gay Street phantom. There are probably dozens on the tiny street where a morgue from the Revolutionary War era was once located. Gay Street, said to have been named for the abolitionist and editor Sidney Howard Gay in 1833, is one of the oldest streets in New York City. It started out as an alley entrance to stables, with its first row of houses being built on the east side of the street in 1827. The earliest residents of Gay Street were predominantly black servants who worked for wealthy families in nearby Washington Square. The street then became a popular location for black musicians, as well as aspiring artists and writers, solidifying its bohemian reputation.

The four-story townhouse at 12 Gay Street was once owned by New York City's mayor, Jimmy Walker, as well as puppeteer Frank Paris, who designed the original Howdy Doody in the building's basement. Paris's puppet shop was—and allegedly still is—located in the basement, where relics from his days there are said to remain.

This is Gay Street's most well-known haunted house—once a speakeasy called the Pirate's Den, then a private residence, and finally an apartment building. Previous owners, houseguests, and tenants have experienced many types of paranormal activity. Unexplained footsteps are heard going up and down the stairs inside during the night, the smell of fried onions pervades the air when nobody is cooking, shadows are seen sliding up and down the stairways of the building, and full-blown apparitions of a bedecked phantom standing on the front steps are reported even to this day. The jovial ghost, dubbed the Gay Street Phantom, has appeared quite often throughout the apartment building and on the inside stairs and outside entrance. The phantom, wearing a top hat and tails, always smiles before vanishing into thin air. Some suggest that he is an alter ego of Walter B. Gibson's Shadow. Three psychic mediums have been brought in on separate occasions, and all agreed that there is at least one ghost of someone who died violently at the premises, possibly through torture for withholding information—even before the house was ever erected.

The Great Northeast Power Blackout

On November 9, 1965, the northeastern United States experienced its biggest power blackout in history. Just before the series of cascading power outages that rumbled through the region, UFOs were spotted over three major cities of New York State—New York, Rochester, and Syracuse—as well as at Niagara Falls and sporadic towns and villages across the power grid. Many witnesses reported UFOs hovering over the main power distribution stations that served New York City and Long Island just moments before the first power outages began.

At 5:16 P.M., a transmission line from a Niagara power plant on the New York–Ontario border tripped, causing five other lines to open and trip at that facility, thus destabilizing the entire system and setting off a series of overloads and outages at other power plants on the grid. Each facility isolated itself from the main power grid in a vain attempt to compensate for what was happening—all within four seconds. But that act in itself caused a critical imbalance between generation and electrical load, which led to yet more lines opening and tripping at every facility affected. When all was said and done, within five minutes of the first line trip at Niagara, other pockets of the northeastern power grid were brought down, leaving thirty million people from New York, Ontario, New Jersey, Pennsylvania, and parts of New England in the dark for thirteen hours.

Blame needed to be placed quickly on someone for such a significant incident. The investigation was thorough and swift. Perhaps too swift. The results were not wholeheartedly accepted by all. The Federal Power Commission laid blame on a faulty automatic relay device for tripping open at the Niagara generating station, setting the devastating series of events in motion. The commission wouldn't say what caused the relay to trip, however. The part had been examined thoroughly and was found to be functioning properly. A later private investigation by the power industry concluded that the relay had been tripped by a huge surge of power from an unknown source. UFOs, perhaps?

It's a documented fact that before power outages throughout the world, UFOs have been spotted near transmission facilities. One of the most common findings in connection with UFO sightings is that they cause electrical devices to malfunction, short out, or have a surge of power. In the case of the Great Northeast Blackout, UFOs had been spotted near many of the major transmission facilities in the Northeast immediately before the blackout. Hundreds of UFO sightings were reported that night—so many, in fact, that NBC News and the Associated Press ran stories on the sightings the next day. The reports raised the possibility that UFOs could somehow be responsible for the blackout. UFOs had even been reported heading east from Ohio toward New York moments before the whole event began. If that were the case, it's possible they were responsible for the power surge that caused the relay to trip as they passed over the first facility.

The New Amsterdam Theatre

In 1995, Walt Disney and Company took over the city landmark on West Forty-second Street known as the New Amsterdam Theatre, once owned by Florenz Ziegfeld, creator of the famed Ziegfeld Follies. Even before Disney's renovation of the structure, which was originally built in 1903, the famous New Amsterdam Theatre ghost—Olive Thomas, former Ziegfeld Follies girl and Florenz Ziegfeld's mistress—had made a name for herself. Olive wasn't inclined to stick to typical paranormal activity such as making doors open and close, talking in an eerie voice, or causing objects to disappear. The theater's highly visible ghost made her presence known in an unmistakable way, allegedly appearing to many, including after-hours janitorial staff, projectionists, security guards, other employees, and audience members. Sometimes people saw a woman in the balcony late at night, wearing a white gown with sil-

ver trim and holding a medicine bottle in her hand. At least one person glimpsed her onstage, and another watched her float through a window out onto Forty-second Street.

When renovations began in 1995, construction workers reported seeing a beautiful woman wandering about the theater oblivious to them. The fact that she was observed wearing a sash that said "Olive" on it was a dead giveaway to the ghost's identity, although the woman often looked so solid that they had no idea she was a ghost. They didn't know who Olive was, for that matter. But the costume she wore was readily identified as a Follies costume, and she was always holding a mysterious blue glass in her hand.

Former Follies girl Olive Thomas, who had gone on to become a silent film star, died in Paris of mysterious causes in 1920. She was found holding a blue glass in her hand. Later it was reported that she had swallowed bichloride tablets instead of her usual sleeping pills, but nobody knows for certain whether it was accidental, suicidal, or intentional poisoning by someone else at the height of her career. Perhaps if she had swallowed the sleeping pills, she would have been able to rest in peace. But as it was, she died far too young—and was buried in a white gown with silver trim.

There have been no claims of any paranormal activity at the theater for some time now. Perhaps Olive has finally attained her elusive sleep, if she was, indeed, the theater's ghost.

Long Island

SOME OF THE MOST BEAUTIFUL BEACHES, MANSIONS, GARDENS, AND resorts in the world can be found on Long Island. Like the rest of New York City, of which Long Island is technically a part, the 118-mile-long island has a rich history—and therefore an abundance of hauntings. Just ask the unsettled spirits at the old Kings Park Psychiatric Center or the vengeful woman haunting Lake Ronkonkoma. But Long Island has more to worry about than a couple of angry ghosts. People there have witnessed clouds that spit, Men in Black, and even the dreaded Black Dog of Misery.

A Cloud with Attitude

New York State certainly has had its share of unexplained phenomena, and one of the most bizarre was a cloud at Oyster Bay that seemed to have a mind of its own. One summer morning in 1975, Long Island science teacher Tom D'Ercole noticed a dark, basketball-size cloud hovering directly over his house as he was about to climb into his car. Just as he was thinking to himself what a peculiar and angry-looking little cloud it was, the cloud shifted slightly and began to expand, as if inhaling, until it was fully six feet high and a foot and a half wide. As D'Ercole described it, the cloud "floated back and forth across the peak of the roof, changing in shape from a small globular mass to a larger ovoid and finally

becoming an abstract, multi-curved, dark, vaporous 'something.'"
He watched transfixed as the strange meteorological anomaly continued to change before his eyes. To a man of science, it must have
been a truly riveting sight.

Then suddenly the cloud seemed to purse some imaginary lips
before letting loose a direct stream of rain aimed squarely at D'Ercole and his car. After about a minute of carefully directed spray-
ing, the ornery cloud simply vanished. D'Ercole took his soaked
shirt to the junior high school science lab where he worked and ran
a pH test on it. The test revealed that the strange "cloud spit" was
nothing more than typical rainwater.

Kings Park Psychiatric Center

Kings Park Lunatic Asylum started out in 1885 with three wooden
buildings housing fifty-five patients on eight hundred acres of land.
Ten years later, the name was changed to Kings Park Psychiatric
Center, which harbored nine thousand patients in 150 buildings by
1950. In its earliest days, treatment of the insane at Kings Park con-
sisted of the benign yet effective combination of rest, manual labor,
and relaxation. The fresh air and sunshine seemed more therapeutic
than any other treatment available at the time. As the asylum's population rapidly increased, however, other, far more drastic therapies
became popular, such as lobotomies and shock and insulin therapies. By 1950, psychiatric drugs became the treatment of choice for
mental patients. The need for long-term care of psychiatric patients
decreased as various drugs became available that enabled patients
to function within their communities. In 1996, the colossal psychiatric center was shut down and vacated, and portions of the grounds
were turned into a state park. Though the dilapidated, creepy-look-
ing structure appears to be abandoned, many people believe it's
infested with tormented souls from its most brutal days. Those poor
souls may be sharing their space sometime soon, if plans go forward to use the buildings for government offices.

In the tunnels, where remnants of torture chambers are said to
exist, paranormal activity appears to be highest. There people have
felt cold spots as unseen hands pushed on them, and heard loud

banging and clanging echoing through the corridors. Many have reported feeling as if they were being watched. In the old medical building, people have seen misty forms manifesting into apparitions and strange lights shining through the windows. Sobs emanate from Wisteria House, Building 15. The burial grounds near the center of the property, where scores of patients were laid to rest, harbors one particular ghost that chases trespassers away—a far more effective technique than the No Trespassing signs could ever be.

More Men in Black

When the movie *Men in Black,* starring that irresistible duo Will Smith and Tommy Lee Jones, was released in 1996, the connection among UFOs, aliens, top-secret government agencies, and the enigmatic Men in Black instantly achieved large-scale recognition. But as ufologists use the term, Men in Black are not government agents assigned to seek out and destroy alien life forms and erase the public's knowledge thereof. Rather, they are thought to be alien life forms *disguised* as government agents, assigned to seek out and understand humans—while at the same time encouraging them (as only impostors of top-secret government agents can) to forget the UFOs they invariably saw prior to their paranormal visit.

The enigma of men dressed in black who are somehow associated with UFO cover-ups seems to have taken hold in 1953, when the founder of the International Flying Saucer Bureau (IFSB), Albert Bender, claimed to have been told by three men from the U.S. government who wore dark suits that it was strongly inadvisable to continue his organization's UFO research, and he urged extreme caution to his comrades who chose to continue the work. He later said that the three agents had explained the mystery of flying saucers to him but threatened him with prison time if he ever repeated a word of what they told him about UFOs. He remained silent for nine years, but then he wrote a book called *Flying Saucers and the Three Men,* which had a huge impact on the popular image of the Men in Black, and he said that the three men had materialized in his bedroom. If true, it was a point that made it likely there was something paranormal about the Men in Black who paid him a visit. Even today the government hasn't reached the point of beaming people up and down like that—unless there's something it's not telling us.

In all of New York State, Long Island seems to be the "home" where the Men in Black roam. There are only about forty well-documented cases of potentially real encounters, one of which happened in the 1990s to a resident of Mount Misery. A woman was approached by two men (some accounts say four) who looked to be of Indian heritage, with high, strong cheekbones and dark complexions. Though it was pouring rain and the hill they ascended toward her home was muddy, the men's shoes somehow remained completely dry. They proceeded to ask the woman questions that were both trivial and personal, and then they told her she was in possession of their property and they were going to get it back. Mount Misery is a known hot spot for UFO sightings, and some who would research the local phenomena have been thwarted in their attempts to uncover the truth. In the 1960s, a Woman in Black visited a Long Island family shortly after they had reported seeing a UFO in the area. She pretended to be a reporter from a Long Island newspaper there for an interview and asked the family a series of personal questions—not the type they were expecting about their experience. After the strange woman left, the family discovered that the newspaper had no employee by that name.

Most sources agree on certain characteristics of the typical encounter with Men in Black. The men are usually described as having Asian or Indian features, olive complexions, slanted eyes, and thin lips pursed in dead serious expressions; attire consisting of brand new, though outdated, black suits, sunglasses, and black hats; and speaking in a monotone and moving in a mechanical manner, having difficulty choosing their words and performing simple tasks such as eating with a spoon or writing with a pen. They tend to travel in groups of two to four and claim to belong to a government agency, briefly flashing identification badges. The names they give are never found within the agency they claim to represent. They show up at houses where the residents have recently seen UFOs and usually warn them not to report their encounter, and they ask inappropriate personal questions. Based on all recorded accounts of encounters, Men in Black typically drive large, black cars, such as Lincolns, Cadillacs, or Buicks, and they are in mint condition even though they appear to be at least twenty years old.

John Keel, a New York author and Men in Black researcher and expert, has chronicled encounters all over the Northeast. He has

---

had his own experiences with Men in Black, such as when black Cadillacs seemed to be following him on Long Island. He turned around and gave chase, but these pursuits always ended with the mysterious Cadillacs vanishing into thin air somewhere on dead-end roads. At least they didn't attempt to run over Keel, as they tried to do to another UFO witness on Long Island.

Keel researched another Long Island case where two men threatened two different UFO witnesses with a revolver, claiming to be with the U.S. Air Force and telling them to watch out whom they spoke to about their sighting. Three other Long Island residents were interviewed by a supposed Air Force colonel, who had them fill out long questionnaires regarding their personal lives. The Air Force later denied having any employee by the name the alleged colonel was going by. He was a man of many faces, because shortly thereafter, he was spotted in the same neighborhood taking photographs of the homes of those he had interviewed, but now he was wearing a postman's uniform.

Keel has long believed that the Men in Black are not government agents, but supernatural beings somehow associated with the UFOs, and no wonder. People who have been paid visits by these mysterious beings consistently marvel over the Men in Black's knowledge of their personal lives, including details about their relationships that these strangers couldn't possibly have known and particulars about their UFO encounters that they had never mentioned to anyone—as if the Men in Black had been inside of, or very near, the UFOs that were seen by the witnesses.

So are they aliens or government agents? Like all things paranormal, until a Man in Black can be captured and analyzed, we can't even prove they exist, let alone identify what they are. They've got a good cover going for them, whoever or whatever they are.

Mount Misery

Mount Misery is off Sweet Hollow Road in Huntington, Long Island, and was so named by early settlers, who had a devil of a time traversing the woody precipice with their horses and wagons. So many gruesome and bizarre legends have become associated with it that even with the advent of motor vehicles making passage much easier, driving on this narrow, forested stretch can still be a miserable—and downright terrifying—experience. And Sweet Hollow Road is no sweeter.

Not only do Mount Misery and Sweet Hollow Road have many ghost stories associated with them, but they also have tales of Men in Black, the Black Dog of Misery, a phantom policeman, UFO sightings, and a gravity hill. The bulk of the ghost stories are blamed on a hospital located on top of Mount Misery that was burned to the ground in 1851 by either an insane woman or a deranged nurse. When a new hospital was rebuilt, it too burned down. Since then, some have seen spirits running and screaming from the grounds, as if they were fleeing the burning hospital. Others have seen apparitions of various women—one in a red gypsy outfit, another appearing to be a nurse, and a lady in white dubbed Mary, who is the one seen most often. Mary has also been seen at the nearby cemetery and jumping out in front of cars on Sweet Hollow Road. Some believe she was a depressed patient who set the hospital afire, then died in the flames along with others. Others think she was either killed in an accident on that stretch of road or murdered. No existing documents shed any light on her identity, unfortunately.

Besides Mary, there is also a phantom police officer said to appear fairly solid, but with a blood-stained uniform. When he turns around, the back of his head is missing. Urban legend? Perhaps. It's about as believable as the escaped mental patient said to kill teens using Mount Misery as a make-out spot with his prosthetic hook. There's another story about multiple apparitions hanging from the Northern State Bridge and overpass, where a group of kids hanged themselves in a suicide pact in the 1970s. If you honk your horn three times, the story goes, they'll manifest. It's also said that if you park beneath that same overpass and put your car in neutral, it will somehow be pushed uphill—against gravity.

Mount Misery is also considered a hot spot for UFO activity. In the 1990s, there were so many sightings in the area that a group called Island Skywatch set up a UFO hotline. Finally, there is the Black Dog of Misery—something you never want to encounter. Throughout the world, large black dogs, or "hell hounds," are feared in areas where paranormal activity abounds, because they are believed to be harbingers of death. He who sees one of these elusive canines, with their red, glowing eyes, is being warned of his impending death. There is said to be such a dog somewhere on Mount Misery. Pray you don't see him.

The Lady of the Lake

Lake Ronkonkoma is a kettle lake, a massive bowl-shaped impression caused by the melting of a glacier some twenty thousand years ago, and the largest on Long Island. An old Native American legend of a scorned young Indian chief, who despondently paddled to the middle of the lake, dove deep, and never returned to the surface, led to the misconception that the lake was bottomless. This was believed until 1956, when that myth finally was disproved by a team of divers. In reality, its greatest depth is just sixty-five feet. But the ominous designation attached to it for centuries undoubtedly spawned an assortment of other myths and legends, including those of the Lady of Lake Ronkonkoma, an apparition said to shamelessly lure young men to the depths, from which they would never emerge. There are at least three distinct legends associated with the lake. Though different, all share the same tragic outcome: One young man or boy is said to drown under mysterious conditions in the lake every summer.

In one popular version of the legend, an Indian princess named Ronkonkoma met a prince from another tribe across the lake, and they fell in love. When her parents learned of the affair, they forbade Ronkonkoma to see the man, because he wasn't one of their own. But nothing would stop the young lovers from trying to meet. One night the prince tried to swim across the lake to see her, but he drowned. Ronkonkoma swam out looking for him, and she too drowned. Neither of their bodies was ever recovered. The story goes that each year, the forlorn princess returns to the surface and claims the life of at least one teenage boy in vengeance for the lost love for whom she is still searching.

Another legend has the heartbroken Indian princess rowing out to the middle of the lake, tying weights around her ankles, then slipping over the side and drowning. Her tribe thereafter believed that her restless spirit haunted the lake, causing mysterious waves and whirlpools, and uttering eerie cries into the night for centuries. Many believed she appeared as a solid, alluring young woman at the side of the lake, beckoning trusting young souls to follow her into the water, and ultimately leading them to their deaths.

A third legend omits the Lady of Lake Ronkonkoma altogether, and instead speaks of a curse put on the lake by one of the warring Native American tribes on either side. Every year until eternity, it was said that a male child will drown in the lake.

In the 1970s, a *Newsday* reporter painstakingly researched old newspaper clippings from the area to see if there was any truth to the legend of males drowning each year. Interestingly, there was. It seems that for quite a consecutive number of years, at least one young male actually did drown in the lake. But were the victims truly lured by paranormal means to their demise, or were the number of drowning deaths statistically typical for a lake as large and popular as Ronkonkoma?

As is often the case in questions pitting science against the paranormal, the answer may be lying just beneath the surface, or it may never be known.

Bibliography

Books

Bartholomew, Robert, Paul Bartholomew, William Brann, and Bruce Hallenbeck. *Monsters of the North Woods.* Utica, NY: North Country Books, 1992.

Beckley, Timothy Greene. *The UFO Silencers.* New Brunswick, NJ: Inner Light, 1990.

Clark, Jerome. *Unexplained!* Canton, MI: Visible Ink Press, 1999.

Hauck, Dennis William. *Haunted Places: The National Directory.* New York: Penguin-Putnam, 2002.

Hopkins, Bud. *Intruders.* New York: Ballantine Book, 1987.

———. *Witnessed.* New York: Pocket Books, 1997 (reprint).

Hynek, Dr. J. Allen, Philip Imbrogno, and Bob Pratt. *Night Siege: The Hudson Valley UFO Sightings.* New York: Ballantine Books, 1987.

Irving, Washington. *The Sketch Book of Geoffrey Crayon, Gent.* New York: Signet, 1820.

Jones, Louis Clark. *Murder at Cherry Hill: The Strang-Whipple Case, 1827.* Albany, NY: Historic Cherry Hill, 1980.

———. *Things That Go Bump in the Night.* Syracuse, NY: Syracuse University Press: 1983. Reprint edition.

Macken, Lynda Lee. *Empire Ghosts.* Forked River, NJ: Black Cat Press, 2004.

Myers, Arthur. *The Ghostly Register.* New York: McGraw-Hill/Contemporary Books, 1986.

New York State Road Atlas. Maspeth, NY: Hagstrom Map Company, 2001.

New York State Travel Guide, 2004. New York State Department of Economic Development, 2004.

Pitkin, David J. *Ghosts of the Northeast.* New York: Aurora Publications, 2002.

———. *Saratoga County Ghosts.* New York: Aurora Publications, 1998.

Revai, Cheri. *Haunted Northern New York.* Utica, NY: North Country Books, 2002.

———. *More Haunted Northern New York.* Utica, NY: North Country Books, 2003.

———. *Still More Haunted Northern New York.* Utica, NY: North Country Books, 2004.

Rogers, Melodie. *Followed by Death.* Frederick, MD: PublishAmerica, 2004.

Sharlow, Christopher. *Shutter.* Bloomington, IN: Authorhouse, 2004.

Singleton, Esther. *Historic Landmarks of America.* New York: Dodd, Mead, 1907.

Skinner, Charles M. *Myths and Legends of Our Own Land: The Hudson and Its Hills.* Philadelphia: J. B. Lippincott, 1896.

———. *Myths and Legends of Our Own Land: The Isle of Manhattoes and Nearby.* Philadelphia: J. B. Lippincott, 1896.

———. *Myths and Legends of Our Own Land: As to Buried Treasure and Storied Waters, Cliffs, and Mountains.* Philadelphia: J. B. Lippincott, 1896.

Smitten, Susan. *Ghost Stories of New York State.* Auburn, WA: Ghost House Books, 2004.

Streiber, Whitley. *Communion: A True Story,* revised. New York: HarperCollins Publishers, 1988.

Winfield, Mason. *Spirits of the Great Hill.* Buffalo, NY: Western New York Ware, 2001.

Zarzynski, Joseph. *Champ: Beyond the Legend.* Utica, NY: North Country Books, 1985.

Online Sources
(in Order by Story)

"Beardslee Castle: Inspired American Cuisine." *Beardslee Castle.* Retrieved 28 January 2005. www.beardsleecastle.com/.

"Beardslee Castle." *Dupont Castle.* Retrieved 20 January 2005. www.dupontcastle.com/castles/beardslee.htm.

"Historic Buildings of Herkimer County: Beardslee Castle." *Beardslee Castle, Herkimer County, NY.* Retrieved 20 January 2005. www.rootsweb.com/ ~ nyherkim/manheim/beardslee.html.

"Our Visit to a Haunted Cider Mill . . ." *Unsolved Mysteries.* Retrieved 7 March 2005. www.unsolvedmysteries.com/usm359736.html.

"Champ Becomes a Celebrity." *Lake Champlain Region.* Retrieved 20 September 2004. www.lakechamplainregion.com/content_pages/champy2.cfm.

"Champ History: From Ancient Times." *Lake Champlain Region.*

Bibliography

Retrieved 20 September 2004. www.lakechamplainregion.com/
content_pages/champyhistory.cfm.

"Champ History: Modern." *Lake Champlain Region.* Retrieved
20 September 2004. www.lakechamplainregion.com/content_pages/
champyhistory2.cfm.

"The Champ Search Continues." *Lake Champlain Region.* Retrieved
20 September 2004. www.lakechamplainregion.com/content_pages/
champyscience2.cfm.

"The Possible Science of Champ." *Lake Champlain Region.* Retrieved
20 September 2004. www.lakechamplainregion.com/content_pages/
champyscience.cfm.

Heath, Dan. "Lake's Legend Lives." *PressRepublican.com News.* Retrieved
20 September 2004. www.pressrepublican.com/Archive/2004/
08_2004/080220046.HTM.

"Followed by Death." Home page. Retrieved 24 September 2004.
home.twcny.rr.com/melrogers/.

"Christopher Sharlow's Ghostphotographer.com" Home page. Retrieved
18 December 2004. www.ghostphotographer.com

"'Ghosts of Old Fort Ontario' Program Set." *The Valley News Online—
Oswego News.* Retrieved 10 March 2003. www.valleynewsonline.com/
News/2002/1019/Oswego_News/076.html.

Sievers, Helen. "Fort Ontario." *Ghosts of the Prairie: Investigation Report:
Fort Ontario.* Retrieved 10 March 2003. www.prairieghosts.com/
ftontrpt.html.

"Ghosts of Fort Ontario." *Syracuse Ghost Hunters.* Retrieved 20 September
2004. pages.prodigy.net/kas9865/_import/pages.prodigy.net/kas9865/
index3.html.

"Skene Manor Castle." *Dupont Castle.* Retrieved 10 March 2003.
www.dupontcastle.com/castles/skeneman.htm.

"The Castle on the Mount." *Skene Manor.* Retrieved 28 February 2005.
www.members.tripod.com/skenemanor/.

"Skene Manor, Whitehall." *New York Ghosts: Ghosts and Legends of New
York State.* Retrieved 10 March 2003. www.newyorkghosts.com/
skenemanor.htm.

Case, Dick. "Who Is Roaming along Seneca Hill?" *Halloween in CNY.*
Retrieved 8 November 2004. www.syracuse.com.

Yablonski, Steve. "Tales of a Haunted Harbor Scares Up a Huge Audience." *Oswego Daily News.* Retrieved 21 March 2001.
www.oswegodailynews.com/content/2000/082800/082800haunted_
harbor.shtml.

Trainor, Joseph. "UFOs Intervene in Operation Desert Fox." *UFO Roundup*
3, no. 51. Retrieved 7 March 2005. www.ufoinfo.com/roundup/v03/
rnd03_51.shtml.

"Ancestors Inn at the Bassett House." Home page. Retrieved 21 March 2001. www.ancestorsinn.com/.

"Syracuse City Hall." *Syracuse Then and Now.* Retrieved 7 February 2005. www.syracusethenandnow.net/Dwntwn/MontgmrySt/CityHall/CityHall.htm.

"Visitor's Center/Cohoes Music Hall." *Mohawk Towpath.* Retrieved 7 February 2005. www.mohawktowpath.homestead.com/files/MillDist.pdf.

"Cohoes Music Hall." Home page. Retrieved 7 February 2005. www.cohoesmusichall.com/.

"Highway 17." *Tangled Forest.* Retrieved 22 February 2005. www.tangledforest.com/states2/newyorkx.html.

"Factual Information about Forest Park Cemetery." *Long Island Genealogy.* Retrieved 20 January 2005. longislandgenealogy.com/forestpark.html.

"Spooked in Forest Park Cemetery." *Ghost Village.* Retrieved 7 February 2005. www.ghostvillage.com/encounters/2003/10292003.shtml.

"Abandoned Jet Kills 3 in Car, 1 in House." *Associated Press* (July 3, 1954). Retrieved 10 February 2005. www.kbmorgan.com/ufofiles/db709.htm.

"Aliens from Space . . . The Real Story behind the UFOs, by Major Donald Keyhoe." *Past Histories* 9. Retrieved 10 February 2005. www.kbmorgan.com/ufos/ufofiles/db709.htm.

"One Rocket Missing." *UP.* Retrieved 10 February 2005. www.kbmorgan.com/ufos/ufofiles/db709.htm.

"Planes' Cockpits Heated." *Uruguay Case.* Retrieved 10 February 2005. www.nicap.dabsol.co.uk/580505se.htm.

"Landmark." *Landmark History.* Home page. Retrieved 21 March 2001. landmarktheatre.org/Landmark/history.html.

"Is There a Capital Ghost?" *New York State Senate.* Retrieved 5 October 2004. www.senate.state.ny.us/sws/kids/ghost.html.

"The Station Restaurant and Sleeping Cars." Home page. Retrieved 9 February 2005. www.ithacastation.com/.

"Belhurst History." Belhurst home page. Retrieved 2 December 2004. www.belhurst.com/belhistory.html.

"Cherry Creek, New York: August 19, 1965." *NICAP Case Directory.* Retrieved 10 February 2005. www.nicap.org/tc-650819dir.htm.

"Devil's Hole." *AOL City Guide: Buffalo: Local Ghost Stories.* Retrieved 9 February 2005. www.digitalcity.com/buffalo/entertainment/article.adp.

Day, Rebecca, and Mike Hudson. "Halloween Tour of Haunted Niagara." *Niagara Falls Reporter.* Retrieved 10 February 2005. www.niagarafallsreporter.com/halloweentour.html.

"Ghostly Sightings and Spirit Experiences." *Eagle Soars.* Retrieved 9 February 2005. eaglesoars.homestead.com/Spirits.html.

Bibliography

"Old Fort Niagara." *Paranormal and Ghost Society.* Retrieved 9 February 2005. www.paranormalghostsociety.org/Old%20Fort%20Niagara.htm.

Ballingrud, David. "Phantom or Phenomenon?" *St. Petersburg Times Online World and Nation.* Retrieved 9 February 2005. www.sptimes.com/2002/10/20/Worldandnation/Phantom_or_phenomenon.shtml.

"The Grand Island Holiday Inn." *Western New York Ghosts and Hauntings Research Society: Local Ghost Lore.* Retrieved 9 February 2005. www.ghrs.org/wnyghrs/local2.html.

Day, Rebecca, and Mike Hudson. "Ghostly Past Lingers at Notorious Haunts." *Niagara Falls Reporter.* Retrieved 9 February 2005. www.niagarafallsreporter.com/ghostly.html.

"Seneca Falls Historical Society." Home page. Retrieved 9 February 2005. www.angelfire.com/ny/sfhistoricalsociety/sfhs.html.

"WNY X-Files." *Online Interview with Mason Winfield.* Retrieved 5 October 2004. www.masonwinfield.com.

"The Town That Killed Itself . . . to Escape Deadly Curse." *Clawfoot People Article.* Retrieved 25 January 2005. members.dandy.net/ ~ getchris/zoar/clawfoot.htm.

"Zoar Valley." *Paranormal and Ghost Society.* Retrieved 25 January 2005. www.paranormalghostsociety.org/Zoar%20Valley.htm.

"Crop Circle News: Articles, Pictures, Information, Theory, History and Research." *Crop Circle News.* Retrieved 10 February 2005. www.cropcirclenews.com.

"Rapid Heating." *Crop Circles Scientific Evidence.* Retrieved 9 February 2005. www.mcn.org/1/Miracles/science.html.

"The Medina Croppies." *Mason Winfield.* Retrieved 9 February 2005. www.masonwinfield.com/ArchiveFiles/June%202002/The%20Medina@20Croppies.htm.

Person, Lenore. "Bannerman Island: A Mystery Island on the Hudson." *Bannerman Island History: A Hudson River Jewel.* Retrieved 26 January 2005. www.hudsonriver.com/bannerman.htm.

Poole, Craig. "Bannerman's: The Haunted Isle." *Haunted Castles in New York.* Retrieved 26 January 2005. www.seakayaker.com/banner.htm.

Bannerman, Jane. "Pollepel: An Island Steeped in History." *Bannerman Castle Trust.* Retrieved 20 January 2005. www.bannermancastle.org/history.html.

"About Christ Church." *Christ Church.* Retrieved 20 January 2005. www.christchurchpok.org/aboutcec.htm.

"Christ Episcopal Church." *The Spirit Realm.* Retrieved 10 January 2005. www.thespiritrealm.com/NY.HTM.

"Ghost Story." *SLMS RevWarQuest: Ghost Story.* Retrieved 5 October 2004. www.kcusd.org/ ~ slorenzo/webquests/revwar/ghost.html.

"Giant Spirit Pig, Other Ghosts Give Name to Fishkill's Spook Hollow." *Haunted Hudson Valley.* Retrieved 5 October 2004. www.pogonews.com/enjoy/stories/haunted1.htm.

Marino, Vivian. "A Real Estate Nightmare: Trying to Sell a Home with Skeletons in the Closet Can Be Scary." *Associated Press: Virginian-Pilot.* Retrieved 20 January 2005. scholar.lib.vt.edu/VA-news/VA-Pilot/issues/1995/vp950704/07040389.htm.

Rothbaum, Rebecca. "Are We Alone?" *Poughkeepsie Journal: News and Sightings.* Retrieved 4 March 2005. www.pinebushufo.com/pinebushpage3.htm.

"Burlingham Inn UFO Bed and Breakfast." Home page. Retrieved 4 March 2005. members.aol.com/ufobb/.

"The Hudson Valley UFO." *The UnMuseum: The Hudson Valley UFO.* Retrieved 10 February 2005. www.unmuseum.com/triufo.htm.

"The Pine Bush Phenomenon." *All about Pine Bush, NY.* Retrieved 4 March 2005. www.pinebushufo.com/pinebushpage1.htm.

"The Real Sleepy Hollow." *Shadowland: Tales from the Shadows.* Retrieved 10 February 2005. home.att.net/ ~ shadowlandhome/sleepyhollow_frame.html.

"Sleepy Hollow." *Sleepy Hollow.* Retrieved 9 February 2005. www.bedofnailz.com/sleepyhollow.html.

"West Point, Room 4714." *HauntedHouses.com.* Retrieved 9 February 2005. www.hauntedhouses.com/states/ny/house6.htm.

"86: Manhattan, NY." *Towns and Tales: 86.* Retrieved 10 February 2005. www.hometowntales.com/86.html.

"Elegant Dinner Served by a Ghost?" *VirtualTourist.com: Staten Island Restaurant Guide: Old Bermuda Inn.* Retrieved 9 February 2005. www.virtualtourist.com.

"Belasco Theatre." *Belasco Theatre: New York City Landmark: JimsDeli NYC Guide.* Retrieved 28 January 2005. www.jimsdeli.com/landmarks/42-51_w/belasco-theater.htm.

"Belasco Theatre." *The Spirit Realm.* Retrieved 27 September 2004. www.thespiritrealm.com.

"The Oldest Drinking Establishment in New York." *Bridge Café Bar and Restaurant.* Retrieved 20 January 2005. www.eatgoodinny.com/.

"The Restaurant They Built a Bridge Over." *Rick Weissman's FunWithWine.com.* Retrieved 1 February 2005. www.bridgecafe.citysearch.com/.

"The Brooklyn Bridge Abduction." *Alien Abductions.* Retrieved 27 September 2004. www.crystalinks.com/abduction.html.

"New Developments in Linda Cortile Abduction." *UFO Updates.* Retrieved 20 January 2005. www.virtuallystrange.net/ufo/updates/2001/aug/m30-022.shtml.

Bibliography

Lloyd, Andy. "The Brooklyn Bridge Encounter." *Cosmic Conspiracies.* Retrieved 27 September 2004. www.ufos-aliens.co.uk/cosmicbrooklyn.htm.

"A Dump with Dignity: The Ear Inn." *James Brown House.* Retrieved 9 February 2005. www.jamesbrownhouse.com/history-earinn.htm.

"History and Highlights from the Book." *James Brown House.* Retrieved 9 February 2005. www.jamesbrownhouse.com/history.htm.

"Speakeasy to Landmark: The Ear Inn Story." *Online News from the Tribeca Trib.* Retrieved 9 February 2005. www.tribecatrib.com/newsfeb03/ear_inn.htm.

"Gay Street." *Frommers.* Retrieved 11 January 2005. www.frommers.com/destinations/newyorkcity/0021020033.html.

"Gay Street, Manhattan." *Wikipedia.* Retrieved 11 January 2005. en.wikipedia.org/wiki/Gay_Street,_Manhattan

"Gay Street, Nos. 14-16." *Museum of the City of New York.* Retrieved 11 January 2005. www.mcny.org/Exhibitions/abbott/a263.htm.

"The Gay Street Ghosts." *New York City Haunted Houses.* Retrieved 5 January 2005. www.hauntedhouses.com/states/ny/house2.htm.

"The Shadow." *Biography of the Shadow.* Retrieved 18 February 2005. members.iquest.net/ ~ drivers/Biog.html.

"The Shadow in Review." Home Page. Retrieved 18 February 2005. www.spaceports.com/ ~ deshadow/.

"The Shadow Old-Time Mystery Radio Show." *Mystery Net.* Retrieved 18 February 2005. www.mysterynet.com/shadow/.

"On November 9th, 1965." *NICAP.* Retrieved 21 January 2005. www.nicap.dabsol.co.uk/nyne.htm.

"The Great Northeast Blackout." *UFOs over Niagara Falls Power Outage Speculation: UFO, April 1968.* Retrieved 10 February 2005. www.mtnet/ ~ watcher/UFOgreatnortheastblackout1965.html.

"Troubled Times: '96 Power Outage." *HAL-PC Internet Services (HALNET).* Retrieved 10 February 2005. www.zetatalk.com/theword/tword07f.htm.

Sellar, Tom, "The Ghosts of 42nd Street." *Roundabout Theatre Company: Front and Center Online.* 13 October 2004. www.roundabouttheatre.org/fc/spring01/ghost.htm.

"Attacked by a Cloud." *Clouds of Suspicion.* Retrieved 1 October 2004. paranormal.about.com/library/weekly/aa011000a.htm.

"Cloud Anomalies." *Clouds: SKYGAZE: Interesting Facts, the Strange and Unexplained, Mysteries and Secrets.* Retrieved 5 October 2004. www.skygaze.com/content/Clouds.shtml.

"Kings Park Ghosts." *Long Island Oddities: Ghosts.* Retrieved 21 January 2005. www.lioddities.com/ghost/kingspark.htm.

"Kings Park Psychiatric Center." *Long Island Ghost Hunters.* Retrieved 9 February 2005. www.longislandghosthunters.com/kings_park.htm.

"Maniacal Laughter." *Long Island Press.* Retrieved 21 January 2005. www.longislandpress.com/v01/i41031023/coverstoryb_01.asp.

"Men in Black (MIB): Not Just a Movie." *Long Island Oddities.* Retrieved 21 January 2005. www.lioddities.com/UFO/mib.htm.

"Men in Black Facts." *UFO Evidence.* Retrieved 5 October 2004. www.ufoevidence.org/documents/doc1701.htm.

"Don't Come Here Alone: Mount Misery, off Sweet Hollow Road, Huntington." *Long Island Press.* Retrieved 21 January 2005. www.longislandpress.com/v01i41031023/coverstoryb_01.asp.

"Long Island Legends: Sweet Hollow Road." *Long Island Ghost Hunters.* Retrieved 9 February 2005. www.longislandghosthunters.com/sweet_hollow_roadhtm.

"Mount Misery and Sweet Hollow Road." *Long Island Oddities.* Retrieved 21 January 2005. www.lioddities.com/ghost/Misery.htm.

"Every Year, Someone Drowns in Lake Ronkonkoma." *Unknown Armies.* Retrieved 11 January 2005. www.unknown-armies.com/content_comments.php?id + 64_0_3_0_C8.

"The Lady of the Lake." *The Haunted Island: Lake Ronkonkoma: The Lady of the Lake.* Retrieved 5 October 2004. www.geocities.com/lighosts/LadyLake.htm.

"The Legend of the Lady of the Lake." *Lady of the Lake.* Retrieved 11 January 2005. www.geocities.co/aardduck/lady.html.

Acknowledgments

I THANK KYLE WEAVER, MY WONDERFUL EDITOR AT STACKPOLE BOOKS, for believing in me and for his expertise and professionalism. Thank you also to associate editor, Amy Cooper, who worked closely with me on this one as well. I applaud artist Heather Adel Wiggins for her clever supernatural designs that grace the covers and pages of this book and *Haunted Massachusetts,* as well as others in this series not written by me. Her intuitive atmospheric artwork always adds the desired spook effect to the stories.

Many thanks to the people who gave me the nod to include their stories in this book or otherwise assisted me along the way. They include, but are not limited to the following:

Randall Brown, Beardslee Castle; Cindy Steiner, Burrville Cider Mill; Christopher Sharlow; Melodie Rogers; Catherine Manuele, Whitehall Skene Manor Preservation, Inc.; Mary Weidman, Ancestors Inn; the Landmark Theatre Board of Trustees; Terry and Barbara Ciaschi, The Station Restaurant and Sleeping Cars; Daniel R. Gilliland, Holiday Inn Grand Island Resort and Conference Center; Hastings Lewiston, Inc.; Frances T. Barbieri, Seneca Falls Historical Society; Chumley's; Marie DaGrossa, Manhattan Bistro; C. Brennan, Old Bermuda Inn; Rosanne Manetta, One If by Land, Two If by Sea; The Shubert Archive; Adam Weprin, the Bridge Café; and Rip Hayman, The Ear Inn, and Joan Szarka.

I'm forever grateful to my parents, Tom and Jean Dishaw, as well as my siblings, Chris Walker, Tom Dishaw, and Cindy "CJ" Barry—the other author in the family. Their love and support is a source of great comfort to me. A big thank you to J. L. Dumas for lending a helping hand so often lately with a myriad of day-to-day tasks, both daunting and trivial . . . helping to entertain a spirited five-year-old comes to mind first (killing the killer ants would have to be a close second). *Muchas gracias* to Leland Farnsworth for his camaraderie, candid advice, and sincere encouragement of the work I do. Without the thoughtfulness of family and friends, this working mother of four could not have met her publisher's deadline, let alone kept her sanity.

Most of all, I thank my daughters, Michelle, Jamie, Katie, and Nicole, for their patience and understanding every time I said, "Not yet. I have to finish writing this manuscript." The book is done, girls. *The kitchen will now reopen!*

About the Author

CHERI REVAI IS THE AUTHOR OF THE BEST-SELLING HAUNTED NORTHERN New York three-book series, as well as *Haunted Massachusetts: Ghosts and Strange Phenomena of the Bay State.* A North Country native, she has always resided in St. Lawrence County, New York, with her family. She is a mother of four, a secretary, and an author who has been interviewed extensively by regional newspapers, magazines, television news programs, and radio shows. Revai enjoys visiting every nook and cranny of her beloved home state.

Other Titles in the
Haunted Series

Haunted Connecticut
by Cheri Revai • 978-0-8117-3296-3

Haunted Delaware
by Patricia A. Martinelli • 978-0-8117-3297-0

Haunted Illinois
by Troy Taylor • 978-0-8117-3499-8

Haunted Jersey Shore
by Charles A. Stansfield Jr. • 978-0-8117-3267-3

Haunted Maine
by Charles A. Stansfield Jr. • 978-0-8117-3373-1

Haunted Maryland
by Ed Okonowicz • 978-0-8117-3409-7

Haunted Massachusetts
by Cheri Revai • 978-0-8117-3221-5

Haunted New Jersey
by Patricia A. Martinelli and Charles A. Stansfield Jr.
978-0-8117-3156-0

Haunted New York City
by Cheri Revai • 978-0-8117-3471-4

Haunted Ohio
by Charles A. Stansfield Jr. • 978-0-8117-3472-1

Haunted Pennsylvania
by Mark Nesbitt and Patty A. Wilson
978-0-8117-3298-7

Haunted Vermont
by Charles A. Stansfield Jr. • 978-0-8117-3399-1

Haunted Virginia
by L. B. Taylor Jr. • 978-0-8117-3541-4

Haunted West Virginia
by Patty A. Wilson • 978-0-8117-3400-4

WWW.STACKPOLEBOOKS.COM • 1-800-732-3669